Hot Rod

MW01098467

Tim Remus & Dennis Overholser

Published by:
Wolfgang Publications Inc.
PO Box 10
Scandia, MN 55073

First published in 1997 by Wolfgang Publications Inc., P.O. Box 10, Scandia, MN 55073, USA.

ISBN number: 0-9641358-6-8

Printed and bound in the USA

On the cover: Greg Ducato's Model A is a real hot rod - no top, no radio and no air conditioning, just a big 425 cubic inch Buick nailhead V-8 and a Turbo 400 transmission mounted in aftermarket frame rails with a Brookville body.

Hot Rod Wiring

From the Publisher

During my years as a mechanic I learned that no matter how good you are, there are times when you just have to ask for help. If what you need is help in writing a book about wiring hot rods and specialty vehicles, then you need someone who is part mechanic, part engineer and part technician. A person, for example, who spends his days at the office designing wiring kits for a large aftermarket company, and his nights in his home shop installing those kits in street rods and old trucks.

Dennis Overholser is the man who designs the components for Painless Wiring. He's the man people call when they've got a really tough problem. His abilities come from a life-time spent hands-on and under the hood, combined with a healthy curiosity and his early electronics training.

Dennis and I approached the book as a partnership. He is the man responsible for most of the words. My job was to massage the words and fill in any blank spaces. The job of photography also fell into my realm, and except where noted all the photographs are my own. My final task was to assemble the 40,000 words and nearly 300 photographs into a finished book.

As publisher, I am grateful to Dennis for all his help and patience. In fact, everyone at Painless helped with this project. Dave McNurlen and Brian Montgomery have to be sin-gled out, however, for taking time out from answering tech calls to answer the endless questions from Tim Remus.

Speaking of helpful people, Greg Ducato must be thanked for providing us with a vehi-cle for the Hands-On installation chapter. Jack Chisenhall, owner of Vintage Air, provided advice for anyone adding air conditioning to their car. And for help with the Gauges chap-ter I must tip my hat to the good people at Auto Meter Gauges. Insights into EFI come from local Corvette specialist Doug Rippie at Doug Rippie Motorsports. Ford Motorsport lent that same chapter a certain balance by providing information on their high perfor-mance fuel injection products.

The Stereo chapter couldn't have been assembled without the input and assistance of Kelly Kitzman at Sound Waves. Another Minnesotan, Bob Peterson provided help with alternator circuits, and my old friend Bob Larsen (aka, Yup) proof read the whole manu-script. Final thanks go to my lovely and talented wife, Mary Lanz, for moral support and for allowing me to ignore family responsibilities during this always frantic holiday season.

Timothy Remus

Introduction

Though this book contains information on basic DC electrical circuits, the idea is to help you install, not design, wiring for your car or truck. Most of the copy, photos and diagrams are intended to answer real-world questions and needs. You don't need to know which way the electrons actually flow through a wire, but you do need to know how heavy the wire should be and where to connect the terminal. The information in this book has been compiled in part from the manuals published by Painless Wiring of Fort Worth, Texas.

We've done our best to address the needs of different parts of the car and truck hobby. Street rods, classic American cars, pickup trucks (old and new) 4X4s and competition vehicles are all discussed here. Though the basic circuits might be the same, the number of circuits needed by a bare-bones hot rod is different from a fancy truck with A/C and power windows.

Because so many people are adding electronic fuel injection to older vehicles we've included a chapter that helps explain how EFI works, what to look for in a harness and how to install that harness.

The other thing that's showing up in new/old vehicles in increasing numbers is "killer stereos." With this in mind we've included a complete chapter on Automotive Audio. The discussion includes what to buy and why. The same chapter walks the reader through a high-dollar installation done on a fancy, late model Firebird.

The book closes with a chapter on Installation Tips and Trouble Shooting. Like the first chapter, the last is written in language anyone can understand. Unlike the other chapters, this one includes a question and answer section put together with help from the technicians who answer the tech line at Painless Wiring.

About Painless Wiring

In 1990 "Painless Wiring" began in a 5000 square foot building as Perfect Performance Products Inc. manufacturing wiring harnesses solely for the street rod and light truck markets. At that point Perfect Performance Products produced only two part numbers.

Today, the new catalog lists literally hundreds of parts and products designed for heavy duty trucks, 4x4's, street rods, late model trucks and many competition applications. The growth of Painless Wiring is based on the production of quality parts designed to answer the needs of real people. The development of these products has resulted in many awards including two for Best New Products of the Year from Specialty Equipment Market Association (SEMA), five runner-up awards from SEMA and a Best New Safety Related Product award from the National Street Rod Association (NSRA).

The name Painless Wiring started as a compliment from an automotive writer after he installed a wiring harness from Perfect Performance Products. The staff at Painless Wiring work to design and build high quality products that can be sold at a fair price - and thus maintain their reputation for developing wiring products that are truly Painless.

Chapter One

Basics of DC Electricity

Where it all starts

It is not our intention to offer an engineering level textbook explanation of DC electronic theory. Rather, this book is intended to serve the individual wiring or rewiring a car or truck. With this end goal, we offer here an overview of electronic theory and a basic explanation of the electronic components most at-home installers are likely to encounter.

Painless Wiring manufactures a variety of wiring harness kits, in both 12 and 18-circuit models. These harness kits come with the wires already attached at the fuse block.

What it is

Electricity, whether it is a streak of lightning from the sky, 110 volts from a wall socket in the house, or the high energy spark that ignites the fuel in your automotive engine, is simply voodoo to most people.

There are a lot of theories on how and in which direction electricity flows through wires. Some state that electrons flow through the wire and some state they flow around the wire. Of course there's the question of which way the electricity really flows, from positive to negative or negative to positive?

To most people the answer is "who cares as long as my car starts and runs."

To better understand some basics of automotive electrical systems and why they are designed the way they are, there are a few basic terms we must first understand and a theory that most people can understand. First, the terms.

Voltage: the force that pushes electrons through a wire (sometimes called the electromotive force).

Current: the volume of electrons moving through the wire measured in amps.

Resistance: the restriction to the flow of electrons measured in ohms.

Most people have heard of the "water through the hose theory," where the water pressure is the voltage, the volume of water is the current and the kink in the hose is the resistance.

We offer another theory, the "park bench" theory.

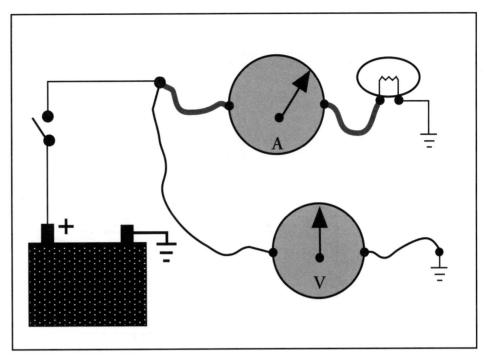

Ammeters and voltmeters are wired in very different ways: ammeters are always hooked up in series, while voltmeters are connected in parallel.

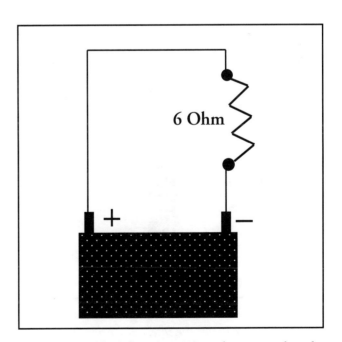

We can use Ohm's law (I=V/R) to determine that the current in this impractical circuit is 2 amps.

7

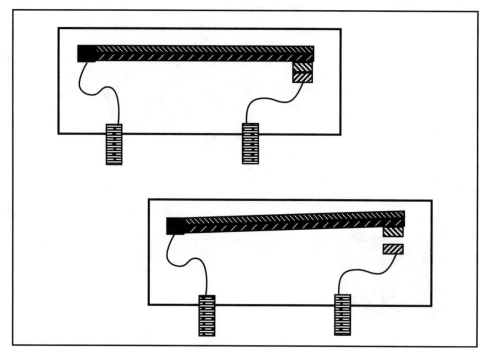

Too much current moving through the bi-metallic strip in this auto-reset circuit breaker creates heat which causes the dis-similar metals to expand at differnt rates.

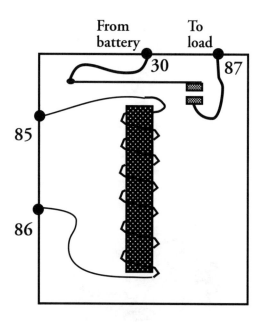

This schematic shows the internal workings of a basic 4-prong electric relay. A small current moving between 85 and 86 (the control side of the relay) creates a magnetic field which closes the load carrying part of the relay.

Voltage (V)

Imagine a park bench, which will represent a wire, just long enough to seat 6 people and each person represents an electron. If someone at one end (the voltage) decides to set down and is large enough to force the 6 people to shift down the bench, a person at the far end will be forced off the bench. This is electron flow.

Current (I)

Current is the number of people (electrons) being moved during a given period of time. Current is measured in amperage (amps) and is controlled by pressure pushing the people on the bench (voltage) and the resistance to their movement.

Resistance (R)

Resistance is the force trying to prevent the people from being forced off the bench. Resistance is measured in ohms.

The way these three forces interact is contained in a very simple formula known as Ohm's law.

Ohm's law: $V = I \times R$ or stated another way, $I = V/R$ and $R = V/I$

To take our earlier example just a little farther, consider that at the end of the bench there's a turnstile and the people going through the turnstile are like current causing an electric motor to rotate. We also need to consider the size of the bench. The bench (which represents the wire) is only intended to hold so many people. If it has too many people on it, it could collapse.

The importance of wire size

The size of wire is very important in the flow of electrons. The larger the wire, with more strands in the wire, the more current it can carry. To relate this to the park bench think of a sport facility where there are rows of benches. Each bench represents one strand of wire - the more strands the more flow. Even though the benches may not always be full of people the potential is there if needed.

Different wire sizes and types are manufactured with different amounts of strands. Most household wire is made of a single heavy strand, good for carrying high voltages and low current. In the automotive applications the wire is sized from light to heavy and is always made up of many strands, which is good for carrying higher current flows at relatively low voltage. Multiple strands also makes the wire flexible and less prone to breakage from vibration.

The size of a wire is known as its gauge. Bigger numbers indicate a smaller wire able to carry a smaller current. A 22 gauge wire might be used for a dash circuit while a 2 or 4 gauge wire would make a good battery cable.

Even within a given gauge, different types of wires will have different numbers of strands. Higher quantity wire generally contains a larger number of smaller diameter strands. As a general rule of thumb, always use the highest number of strands per wire size as possible. A good example of

This TXL wire from Painless uses a very high quality, high temperature insulation that is actually thinner than the insulation on the hardware-store wire most of us are familiar with.

Length / Current	0-4ft.	4-7ft.	7-10ft.	10-13ft.	13-16ft.	16-19ft.
0-20A	14ga.	12ga.	12ga.	10ga.	10ga.	8ga.
20-35A	12ga.	10ga.	8ga.	8ga.	6ga.	6ga.
35-50A	10ga.	8ga.	8ga.	6ga.	6ga.	4ga.
50-65A	8ga.	8ga.	6ga.	4ga.	4ga.	4ga.
65-85A	6ga.	6ga.	4ga.	4ga.	2ga.	2ga.
85-105A	6ga.	6ga.	4ga.	2ga.	2ga.	2ga.
105-125A	4ga.	4ga.	4ga.	2ga.	2ga.	0ga.
125-150A	2ga.	2ga.	2ga.	2ga.	0ga.	0ga.

Wire size chart from the IASCA handbook. The size of wire used in any circuit is determined by the current load and the length of the wire. This chart is for copper wire (don't use aluminum wire).

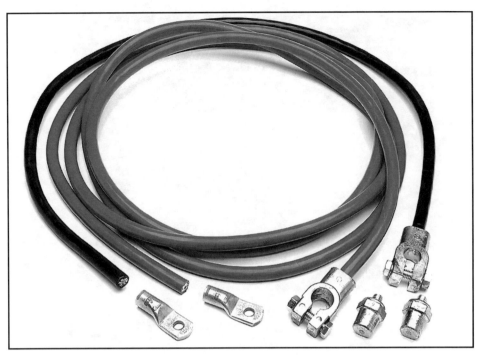

As the battery gets farther away from the starter, the cables must be a heavier gauge. These one-gauge, fine-strand cables from Painless are extra long for trunk mounted batteries.

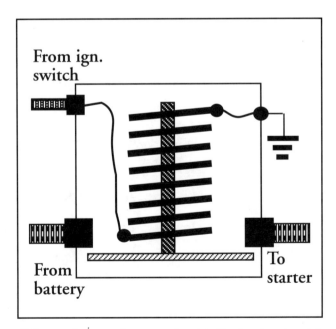

Like a relay on a larger scale, this Ford style solenoid uses a coil of wire to generate a magnetic field and pull the disc up so it provides a circuit between the two large terminals.

this is battery cable. Many people use welding cable for their battery cables because it has much higher stranding than regular battery cable. This results in less voltage drop and heat build-up during use, due to the lower resistance of the multiple strands.

Wire size in a circuit

Charts are available that give the recommended gauge size for a particular situation (see the wire size chart). The two things that determine the gauge needed for a circuit are the current load the wire will need to carry, and the length of the wire that carries that load. More current requires a larger diameter wire (smaller gauge number). The same current, but in a longer piece of wire, will require a larger diameter wire. When in doubt, go larger, not smaller.

The other thing to consider when buying wire is the quality of the insulation. At Painless Wiring we use TXL, with insulation that is thinner, yet more heat and abrasion resistant than anything else on the market.

Remember that the new high temperature insulation like that used with TXL are thinner than the insulation used with lesser grades of wire making it hard to judge the gauge of the wire. What looks at first like a 16 gauge wire might actually be 14 gauge wire with the new, thinner insulation.

CIRCUIT PROTECTION DEVICES

Fuses

A fuse is one of the most important parts of the electrical circuit. The fuse is the weak link in the passage of current and is designed to allow only a preset amount of current to flow through the circuit. By using a fuse, regulation of current flow is possible and damage to sensitive electronic parts and powered circuits can be avoided. A fuse works by having a small conductive strip between the two contacts that is designed to melt at a certain temperature. When current flow reaches a certain maximum level, the natural resistance of the strip creates enough heat to melt the strip, thus stopping current flow. If a wire rubs through the insulation and contacts the frame, the fuse will blow well before the wire gets hot enough to melt. Without a fuse you run the risk of melting the wires in one or more circuits and starting a fire in the car.

Fusible links

A fusible link as used by the factory is a short link of melt-able wire housed in high temperature insulation. Generally used to carry a load heavier than a standard fuse can handle, fusible links are again the weak link in a chain, designed to melt before the wire or circuit itself are damaged. Detroit often uses a fusible link where a large feed wire (eight or ten gauge) connects to the starter solenoid or source of battery power. If the wire with the fusible link in it shorts to ground someplace "down stream" the link will melt preventing the entire wire from burning up.

Diodes

A diode is simply an electronic one-way valve, passing current one way and one way only. The most common use of diodes is in

an alternator, where two banks of diodes are used to convert alternating current to direct current.

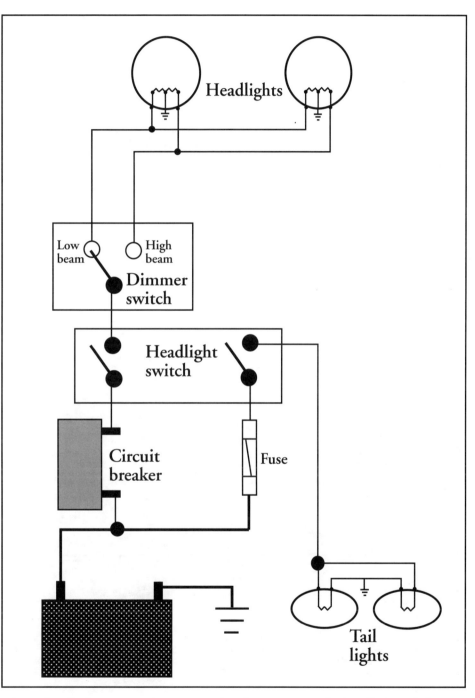

Basic headlight circuit uses a circuit breaker to protect the headlights while a fuse or fuses protect the tail and parking lights.

Circuit Breakers

Circuit breakers, like fuses, are designed to protect circuits from overloading. The major difference between fuses and circuit breakers is that fuses, when overloaded, melt the conductive strip and are not reusable. Circuit breakers, by contrast, have a bimetallic strip that heats up under overload conditions causing a break in the current flow. There are three basic types of circuit breakers being used in automobiles.

Type 1 automatic reset

This type of circuit breaker will automatically reset itself when the bimetallic strip cools. This is the most commonly used type and will continue to turn current off and on as long as the circuit is overloaded. In some type circuits this could be dangerous and damage electronic devices. In a headlight circuit, however, a driver wants the circuit breaker to reset as quickly as possible so the lights are turned back on.

Type 2 automatic reset

This type of circuit breaker will automatically reset only when the overload is removed from the circuit. The bimetallic strip breaks contact like the type 1 but there is a small special resistor along side of the strip which is attached to the contacts. Current passes through this resistor when the main contacts have opened. The heat of the resistor prevents the bimetallic strip from cooling and remaking contact. This type circuit breaker is becoming the preferred choice for electrical system designers because of the higher safety factor.

Manual reset

The manual reset circuit breaker also has the bimetallic strip but it will not reset itself when

Fuses and terminals are color coded to their intended use and optimum current load.

cooled. The strip is pushed back into place, usually with an external button on the circuit breaker housing, and contact of the circuit is remade. This type is most commonly used in electric motors and circuits that have high voltages such as your home or workshop.

CONTROL DEVICES

Relays

A relay can be thought of as a remote switch controlled by another switch. The relay is designed to pass relatively large amounts of current to specific devices, rather than have that current pass through switches and major harnesses. Relays are often used to prevent overloading of circuits, switches and fuse blocks. Simple relays commonly have two circuits, a load circuit that actually carries the heavy load from the battery to the electric fan or pump, and a control circuit that is used to switch the load circuit on and off.

Relays are usually mounted remotely and close to the device that is requiring the extra high current. Power is transferred directly from the battery source to the device through the relay that has been turned on by a switch. In most cases, relays are protected from overloading by circuit breakers.

A good example of a relay would be a horn circuit. When you hit the horn you're usually grounding the control circuit in the relay, which causes the load side of the relay to close allowing current to flow from the battery to the horn. By using a relay there is no need to run the heavy wires needed to power the horn up to and through the steering column.

Solenoids

A solenoid used in a starter circuit is really nothing more than a specialized relay. In the case

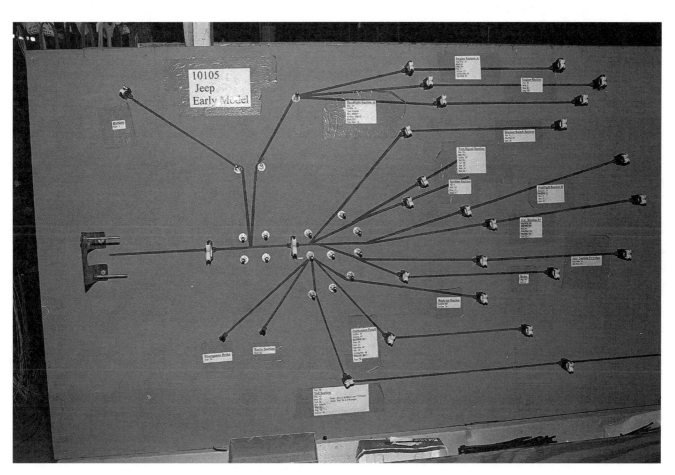

Boards like this one function as "jigs" designed to facilitate construction of a wiring harness at Painless Wiring.

Raw wire is cut and sorted according to color and size, then placed on a cart at one of the assembly stations in the Painless plant.

of a stand-alone solenoid mounted to the fender or firewall, the solenoid is activated by the ignition switch. When the switch is turned to the start position, battery voltage is applied to the coil in the solenoid.

Inside the coil is a movable plunger with a copper disc attached to one end. When the coil is energized, a magnetic field caused the plunger to overcome spring pressure and be drawn into the coil. As this happens the copper disc is brought into contact with two terminals inside the solenoid. One of these terminals is connected to the battery, the other connects to the starter.

In the case of a solenoid attached to the starter, the plunger has an additional task. In addition to moving the copper disc up against the two larger terminals it also moves the starter drive gear into mesh with the flywheel.

Many solenoids of the second type include a second small terminal that is only energized when the starter is activated and can be used as a by-pass for an ignition resistor. Check Chapter Two for more on starter circuits and solenoids.

Though the wires are cut and crimped by machine, much of the actual assembly is still done by hand.

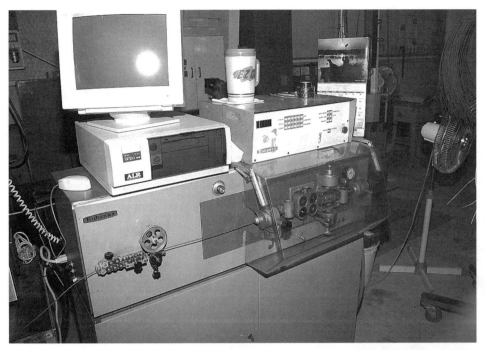

worked there 20 years, the first 14 years as a mechanic and the last 6 as a service manager, which gave me some managerial experience and so forth.

During all those years I had a little shop at the house where I built street rods and custom cars on the side. And I was into drag racing for a while. In 1982 I built my Model A sedan. The next year I drove it to St. Paul, Minnesota, for the Street Rod Nationals in

This machine pulls the raw TXL wire off the big rolls and cuts it to length before terminals are added or the individual wires become part of a harness.

INTERVIEW, DENNIS OVERHOLSER, PAINLESS WIRING

Dennis Overholser is the driving force behind all the products in the Painless Wiring catalog. His training in electronics started in the military, extended through his years as a professional mechanic, and continues to this day with his day-to-day involvement with all aspects of street rodding. Dennis has plenty to say about what makes a good wiring harness and how to re-wire your car or truck with a minimum of time and trouble.

Dennis, why don't you tell me about your background, how the company got started and what your responsibilities are at Painless.

Well, I grew up on a farm and always had some mechanical ability. I built my first car, a '33 Ford, in high school. After high school I joined the military and went through their electronics school and their automotive technician's school. I spent most of my time in the military working in the motor pool. I also got to do some machine shop work and whatever else was needed.

After the military I moved to Texas and started working at the local Ford tractor dealer. I

A printer built on a tiny scale, the head on this machine can print labels on individual wires.

15

Minnesota. I ended up on the NSRA inspection team, eventually I became a rep and then a Division Director for NSRA. So I did that for 11 years. I was real heavily involved there and it opened a lot of doors.

In 1989, I was introduced to Jim Paxton, owner of a van conversion wiring parts company. He was looking for someone to help him break into the street rod and automotive aftermarket with the wiring systems, because the van conversion industry was so volatile. So we got together and I started developing some systems and so forth. The very first thing we built was an 18 circuit kit which we still sell today. We developed it and came out with a couple of part numbers.

We had no more than gotten started when the Gulf War broke out in late 1990 and the van conversion industry went away because of the war. Thank heavens we had some street rod business to help tide us over. So actually that's when Jim and I started Painless Wiring. It was Perfect Performance Products at that time, we didn't have the Painless Wiring logo.

Shortly after that Tex Smith contacted us and did a harness installation story in his magazine, *Hot Rod Mechanix.* Tex said our wiring made the installation painless. So he developed the Painless logo for an ad that we put in the same magazine and it's been used ever since. Now it's become such a household name that we even answer all the phones, 'Painless Wiring.' If I tell somebody I'm with Perfect Performance Products - nobody has a clue what the heck that is.

When we first started the company in 1990 there

All the multi-strand copper wire used in Painless harness kits comes into the plant on these large rolls.

were five of us - Jim and myself and Deana, who is still our plant manager, and two other women. That tells you how we started out.

You've done all the product designs?

Yes, all the product design has been mine since day one. Every product that you see on the shelf, I've either designed or co-designed, so I know how each of them works. That's my responsibility, taking care of all the product development and design.

What makes a good wiring harness or harness kit?

Number one, it's got to be complete. There are so many times you go buy something, especially in the street rod market - you go buy it and it's not all there. You may need some nuts and bolts, or whatever it is, to put it together. My goal is that when you open the box, you don't have to go and buy anything else. Nothing else required. You need a few tools, of course, like everything else. But everything is there, all the terminals and everything you need.

The second thing that I look at - there's lot of different versions of wiring kits out on the market today - and almost everyone does it differently. The majority of the kits start at the fuse block or fuse panel or whatever they want to call it. They tell you to mount it and then attach the wires at the end, like at the headlight or the taillight, and run all

Organized by color and size, these racks hold pre-cut lengths of wire designed for specific kits.

Most of the wires in any good kit are identified by tags. Here the tags have already been added before the wires become part of a harness kit.

17

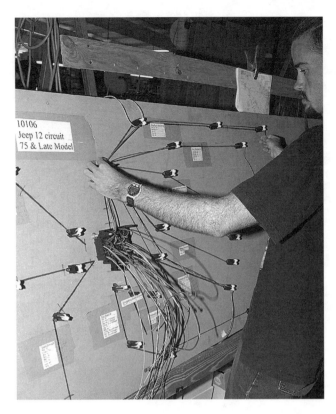

This is how the manufacture of a Jeep wiring harness starts out - individual pre-cut wires of the correct gauge and color are snapped into place on the board.

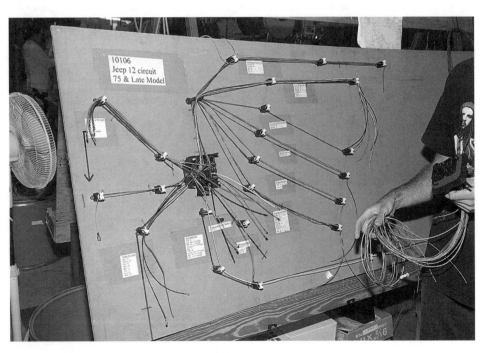

This kit uses a bulkhead connector which is already mounted on the board. The boards automatically organize the wires into the correct circuits.

the wires back to the fuse panel which then becomes a junction block.

Well, we do it a little bit differently. And the reason I do it differently is because number one, up underneath the dash is the hardest place to get too. The seat is in the way, the brake pedal is in the way. So why spend all of the time up underneath the dash? Spend the least amount of time underneath the dash. Let's pre-do all the connections at the fuse block, stick it up underneath the dash, mount it properly, and then run the wires out from there. Once it's mounted, you're physically done. No standing on your head, no removing the seat, no cursing the brake pedal. Then you lay the wires out the way you like them, cut off the excess and terminate them. To me, that's a whole lot simpler.

The biggest enemy to electrical wiring is bad connections. At Painless we make as many of the connections as possible in the factory. The crimps are made by machines and checked with micrometers to be sure they were squeezed just hard enough and not too hard. Then we know all those connections at the fuse box are going to be okay.

The customer doesn't have to worry about that. And it saves a tremendous amount of questions and so forth on the tech line. We don't have to worry about whether or not they hooked the headlight wire to the right terminal on the fuse box.

Are there differences in terms of the quality of the components used in the various wiring kits?

Well, there are some industry standards for components, though different quality kits are available. We get the highest quality components that we can and we strive to have everything American made, because that's what people want. The big difference I guess is in the wire. There's lots of different kinds of wire on the market. If you go down to a local auto supply, you'd get what we call GPT. It's just general purpose wire. For years, we used UL 1015. It's a higher-grade, higher-temperature wire with really heavy insulation, it's excellent wire.

Today, all our wire is TXL. TXL has a very high temperature rating on the insulation, 125 degrees centigrade, but the insulation is a lot thinner so it's lighter in weight and less bulky. This is what the big three are currently using, and all the people that we do business with at NASCAR want TXL because it's lighter weight. So we totally converted over everything that we do to TXL, you can't buy higher quality automotive wire.

When people wire a car, and it's a whole re-wire, what are the typical mistakes they make?

The biggest mistake that most people make is they don't read the instructions. I'm going to say 99 times out of 100 if they read the instructions, they wouldn't be calling us on the tech line. The reason that a lot of people don't read the instructions is because they think they already know how to do the wiring. They've already wired some cars in the past and they think, 'I already know what I'm doing, I don't need to read these.' They probably don't realize that we spend a tremendous amount of time doing the drawings and providing information in the instruction books.

That's probably the biggest problem that we have. As far as any problems that happen, sometimes people get confused. They take the bundle out of the box and they take off some of the informational tags that are on the wires and now they're kind of lost and

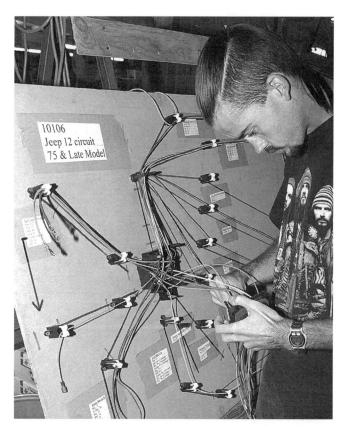

Here you can see most of the wires are in place. Now it's time to add a fuse panel to the fuse block assembly.

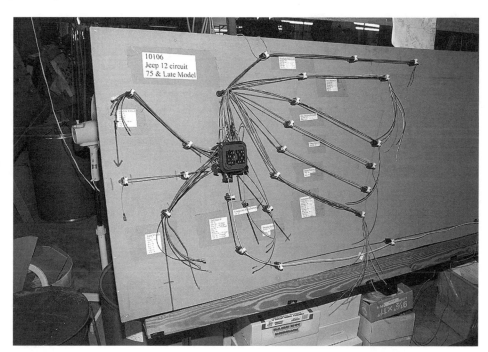

Spring loaded clips hold the wires in group. Before completion each group of wires is tightly wrapped with tie wraps.

Wherever possible the wires are terminated and plug-ins are installed to make the harness as easy to install as possible.

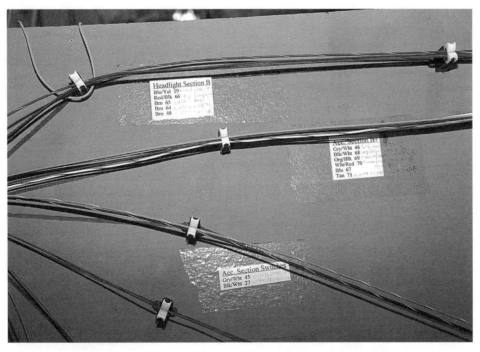

Each assembler has a "cut sheet," a list of the individual wires that make up a kit. In addition, each board is marked with labels to make assembly as foolproof as possible.

they're not sure where one or two wires go.

With fuel injection kits, which we do a tremendous amount of, the questions never end. The biggest problem with that is most people don't understand the basics of fuel injection, why it works, how it works, and what it was designed to do. They may have a problem and because they don't understand it, or they don't know what's going on, they don't have a clue as to how to troubleshoot it. They don't even know where to start. Over the years we've compiled all these questions we get on fuel injection and put the questions and answers into our instruction book. And we try to do it in terms anyone can understand. But still somebody gets confused because a fuel injection harness is very complex. But as far as the number one cause of problems, that would probably be from not reading the instructions.

So there's no reason a reasonably competent individual can't install either a wiring kit or an EFI kit?

That's right, the whole idea is to design the kits to where, especially the EFI kits, everything is a plug in. With the fuel injection kits, if there's a wire that does not have a terminal already on the end, and a good example is a fuel pump wire, the only reason it doesn't is because we don't know how long to make that wire because we don't know where that customer has mounted the fuel pump. So he stretches the wire out, gets it where it should be, cuts off the excess and then terminates it. But all the injectors, all the sensors, the computer, everything has a terminal. If it's possible we go ahead and pre-terminate the end.

That's a little unlike our regular harness because the only thing we pre-terminate on our main harnesses are the terminals for the fuse block and some of the switches. But as far as the light switch connections to the headlights and taillights and turn signals we don't know if it's going to be an Isetta that's six feet long or if it's going to be a '42 Cadillac that's 19 feet long. We provide plenty of wire and leave it up to the customer to lay out the wires the right way, cut off the excess and install the terminals.

Do you have any tips for a typical harness installation?

The first thing I tell the customer, if it's a rewire job, 'have you taken all of the old wiring out of the vehicle?' That's the best thing to do. The reason we recommend that is because it avoids the confusion. You've got a couple of old wires hanging down that they didn't take out and

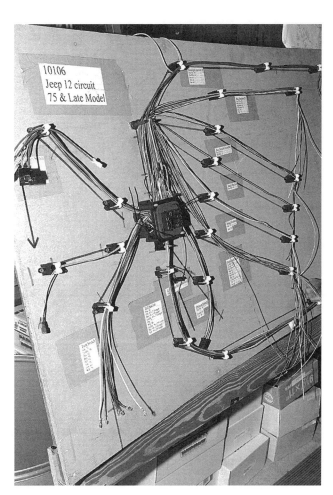

Wires are added one at a time in a predetermined sequence until the harness kit is complete.

Close up shows the fuse block on this nearly completed 12 circuit kit.

then they want to tie them in and they wonder, 'do I tie it in here or here?' If there's nothing in there, there's no questions about what wire goes where or how to tie everything together. So that's the first thing we recommend. Get everything stripped out and get it clean, and then start from scratch. Mount the fuse block, and run the wires, there's three groups: one group goes to the front, one group to the dash, the other group goes to the tail section - it's just that simple. Lay them out the way you want, cut off the excess, and install terminals.

Do you like to see wires soldered or not? Like when I run the wires up to the headlight group?

I have nothing against soldering wires. In fact, there's two ways to look at it. Number one, if you were building a television set that's going to be sit-

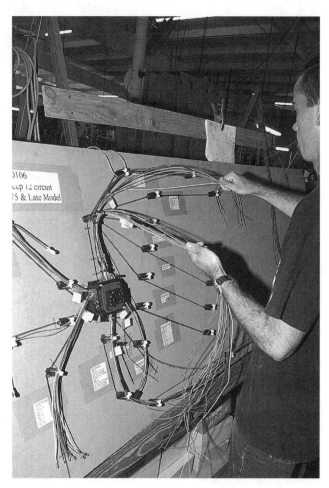

Wires are combed and organized during the assembly to keep everything as neat as possible.

one and the odds are it's not going to break, and the crimp does have a little bit of strain relief built into it. That's why they're a little bit longer than they actually need to be. For everyday use, use a good quality crimp terminal and use a good quality crimp tool, but if you're a professional and you use a soldering iron everyday in your work or whatever and you know the proper way to do things, that's great. Solder and heat shrinks great. Otherwise people should use a crimp connector. That's why we provide good high-quality crimp connectors in all of our kits.

You said people have trouble with grounds and relays. Do you want to touch on those topics?

One of the questions we get is, 'when I turn on the light switch or the turn signals or whatever, the instruments tend to go crazy.' This is a very common problem and usually it's caused by a bad

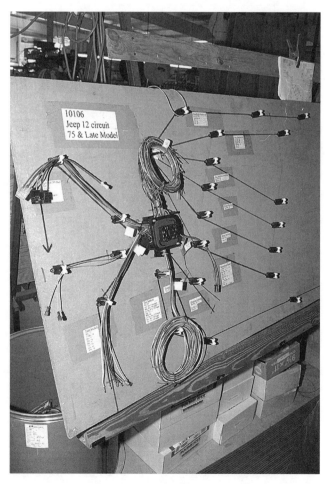

As the circuits are completed each is pulled out of the clips and wrapped into a coil.

ting there in your living room and not moving around and not vibrating, everything else, there's only one way to go. That's solder everything in it. In an automobile, it's a whole different situation. The big factor in soldering in automotive use is - who does the soldering? A factory trained person or someone who's never soldered before.

You take an average Joe on the street that probably has a soldering iron in his hand once or twice a year, maybe, the first thing he's going to do is overheat the terminal. He does not know how to make solder flow. And when he doesn't know how to make the solder flow, then he overheats everything and the wire tends to crystallize. Once the wire crystallizes it takes just very little flex, and the wire breaks so it didn't do any good to solder it. So in the average installation we highly recommend just using crimp terminals. You can crimp ground. The indicator light that's trying to operate in the dash has a bad ground, so it grounds through something else that does have a good ground, like the gauges.

The other problem is that people don't ground the body. Let's say you put your battery in the trunk or a remote location and you run the battery cable down to the frame and bolt it on there. That's wonderful but people forget to tie the body and engine to the frame. The engine can't ground through the motor mounts and the body's sitting on rubber pads. You have to have a ground strap or cable between the battery, frame and engine; and at least a ten gauge wire grounding the body. Good grounds like this will prevent a tremendous number of problems.

The second most common problem area involves the use of relays to power high current devices such as electric fans, electric fuel pumps, or anything that's going to be a real high current draw item. If you try to supply all the power necessary to operate those devices through the fuse block, what sometimes happens is you're trying to consume more than the fuse block and internal circuitry of the fuse block can handle. Sometimes you get a tremendous voltage drop. If you check one of the affected circuits with a volt meter, you'll notice that the reading went from 13.2 volts to 10.1 or 9.8.

Then most people figure the charging system is not working, but that's not necessarily the case. The charging system may be doing just wonderful supplying power to the battery, but the internal circuitry or fuse block is not capable of handling all the amperage necessary to fulfill the needs of the devices drawing current through the fuse block. What we do then is add a relay. A relay is a

Packaging of the finished harness includes all necessary hardware and a thorough set of instructions.

simple electronically controlled switch so the power that would normally go through a key switch or through a toggle switch is now transmitted through the relay. We take power directly from the battery source, it goes through the relay to the cooling fan or fuel pump or whatever. The relay is turned on and off by a remote switch.

By using the relay you eliminate the voltage drop. A big part of the current load is taken off the fuse block. The customer can see that the charging system is working fine and it was working fine all along.

If I've got an old car, like pre-1956 and I want to keep some of the 6 volt components, the gauges maybe, what's the easiest way to do that?

Gauges and radios require a fixed voltage. The only way you can do that is by way of an electronic voltage regulator. There are a couple different ones being made on the market (Painless discon-tinued the manufacture of these units). But usually they consist of a simple solid state circuit and a heat sink. What we're doing is bringing in 12 volts, grounding out six of the volts and allow six of the volts to continue out. A lot of people have tried using ceramic-type resistors to cut the voltage down, and they won't work because a resistor cuts down voltage by heat, and it takes a lot of current flow to produce enough heat to increase the resistance enough to cut the current flow down. Like an ignition resistor - they get extremely hot and they work great, because they're pulling five, maybe ten, amps no problem. You take a gauge or series of gauges that are pulling milliamps, the resistor will never pull enough current to get hot and to make the resistance to drop the current flow. So you can't do it. That's why the electronic style voltage converter is the only way you can do it. They work great. A lot of people use them. The

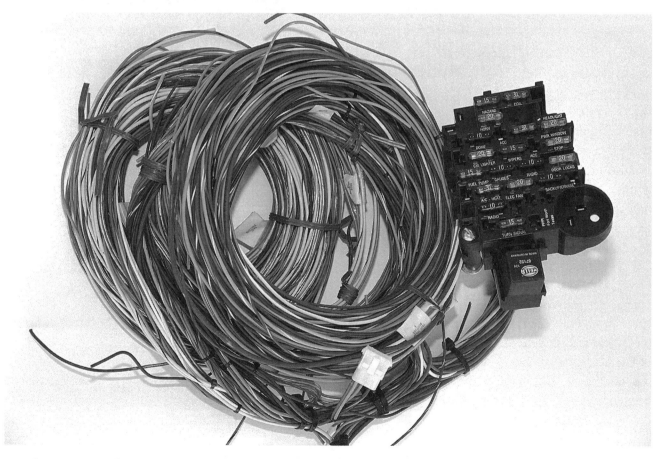

Painless wiring makes a variety of harness kits, both 12 and 18 circuit, that ship complete with all necessary wires already attached to the fuse block.

24

only downfall to these is the current output. Most of them are only rated to five amps so you can run the gauges and the radio fine, but if you want to run the wiper motor or a heater motor then you have to go back to the ceramic resistor.

Are there any tips you want to pass on to people before they jump out there and do their first rewiring job?

The number one thing you have to have to do a wiring job is patience. If you can read, understand drawings, understand color codes or whatever it might be, that's all great. The key is having the patience to sit down and not get in too big a hurry. Don't say, 'I'm just going to go ahead and run this wire over here because I want to hear it run,' and forget about the rest of the car. The first thing you know, you will have that wire and all the other wires going in different directions, and then you think, 'I wish I'd have waited because now my wires are too short.'

There's a lot of redundancy in a wiring job. You're going back over the same group of wires four or five times, running a wire, doing this or that. Run a wire, crimp a terminal, run a wire, crimp a terminal, and on and on and on. It gets boring sometimes. It's not near as much fun as bolting on a set of billet wheels. The flash is not there. But if you don't do it right the first time, you're stuck on the side of the road

and those new Boyds wheels won't do you any good. Patience. Follow the instructions, and it's amazing the number of people who call in and say, 'I've never done one before, I did it and it started the first time.' It was supposed to start the first time.

......It's simple, and a lot of people try to make it harder than it actually is.

More at home in a shop than an office, Dennis Overholser is the man responsible for the design of all Painless Products.

Chapter Two

Batteries, Starters, Alternators

Heart and Soul of the System

Like everything else, the world of batteries, starters and alternators is changing as we speak. New battery designs are announced by the major manufacturers on a regular basis. Some of these new energy cells have a number of advantages, especially for a hot rod or specialized vehicle.

Starters and alternators are evolving too. On the starter front, the mini starter offers more torque in a smaller package than anything offered by Detroit. Alternators have gone from the 40 or

In the case of your alternator, beauty is more than skin deep. What you want is enough output to run the car and the accessories, and keep the battery charged. How well the alternator does its job is determined by what's inside the case.

50 amp models many of us grew up with, to standard outputs of well over 100 amps. High output and aftermarket examples are now available with outputs of double that figure.

This chapter is intended to give you an introduction to the ways in which each component, battery, starter and alternator, operate. New designs are explained with an eye toward our specialized end use. With more understanding of how each component operates you are in a better position to buy something appropriate for your individual needs.

Batteries come in low maintenance and no maintenance designs. Not all no maintenance batteries are truly sealed. The new Optima batteries, a recombinant design, are sealed and can be mounted in any position.

BATTERIES

The heart of any vehicle electrical system is the battery, not only a power source, but also a regulator of voltage in the electrical system.

The battery in your car serves three major functions.

1. The battery is an electricity producing device. The chemical reaction between the lead plates and the electrolyte, a water and sulfuric acid mix, creates electrical current. The voltage is determined by the number of cells.

2. The battery is also a storage device. The battery can store a large amount of current in its plates and is capable of providing this current to the electrical system on demand.

3. The battery is also a regu-

"Marine" battery cases make it easy to mount the battery in the trunk or even inside the car. Be sure to vent the box (unless the battery is sealed or has its own vent hose).

This kit is designed to mount an alternator, power steering pump and A/C compressor to a small block Chevy. Painless Wiring

For special situations there are some very small, yet powerful, batteries on the market - though you might have to adapt your cables to non-standard terminals.

lator of current in the system. As the engine rpm or system loads increase or decrease, the voltage and current flow go up and down. The battery acts as a buffer to damp out spikes and stabilize voltage in the system.

There are two basic configurations for automotive batteries: top post and side post. The top-post style has been around forever. The two lead posts are tapered, typically the positive post is slightly larger in diameter than the negative post.

The side-post battery was developed to help solve several problems. Because the posts are not next to the caps or vents, a source of acid fumes, corrosion of the terminals is reduced. The added benefit of the side post terminal location is the lowered silhouette which allows the batteries to fit more easily into modern cars with lowered hood lines.

Batteries carry a number of ratings, the two most common include cold cranking amps and reserve capacity. Cold cranking amps is the amount of current the battery can provide for a certain length of time at a given temperature. To determine the rating a battery is chilled to zero degrees Fahrenheit and placed under a load in amps for 30 seconds while maintaining a voltage of 7.2 volts. The larger the rating number, such as 500 / 600 /

750, the more power that battery can put out to start your vehicle.

The reserve capacity rating is a means of determining how long a battery might supply current in a situation where the charging circuit has failed. This is the length of time, in minutes, that a fully charged battery can be discharged at 25 amps without allowing the individual cell voltage to drop below 1.75 volts.

BATTERY BASICS

Construction

Automotive batteries are constructed of positive and negative plates kept apart by separators, grouped into cells, connected by straps and suspended in a solution of electrolyte. Though standard wisdom would suggest batteries with longer warranties are built with more plates, a Delco engineer explained that the situation is more complex than that. Batteries with the longest warranties actually have a plate of slightly different type than a battery with a shorter warranty, and the plates themselves might actually be thicker so fewer of them could fit into the battery case.

Each cell of the battery produces approximately two volts, by connecting six cells in series a 12 volt battery is created.

Safety warning

Nearly all batteries emit hydrogen gas, explosive to say the least. Gassing is espe-

The typical G.M. starter includes a solenoid mounted on top which has the job of establishing a connection between the battery and starter, and pulling the starter drive into engagement with the flywheel.

This typical Ford starter is able to engage the starter drive with the flywheel without the help of a solenoid mounted on the starter.

Hot starters sometimes won't crank, especially G.M. designs. These Hot Start systems are designed to eliminate the problem. Painless Wiring

On the left, a Ford starter solenoid and on the right, a G.M. design. Though they may look the same, not all Ford solenoids wire the control side in the same way.

cially likely when the battery is being charged by an external charger but also when the battery is under a load. For these reasons cigarettes, sparks and flames must be kept away from the battery. When jump starting a car be sure the last connection to be made is the negative cable, connected to the frame or engine block of the car being jumped. That way any spark occurs away from the battery.

Wrenches laid on the battery have the potential to short across the terminals and create an explosion. Also remember that metal jewelry conducts electricity at least as well as a wrench (silver and gold are both excellent conductors), which is one more reason to take off the watch and rings before you start work on the hot rod. Remember too that batteries contain sulfuric acid, corrosive to metal and damaging to human skin. Spilled acid should be flushed thoroughly with water.

Battery Chemistry
The plates of the battery are made of lead alloys. Specifically the positive plates are made of lead peroxide while the negative plates are made of sponge lead. These plates are suspended in a solution made up of sulfuric acid and water. When the battery discharges, sulfate (sulfur and oxygen) from the electrolyte combines with the lead on both the positive and negative plates.

As these sulfur compounds are bound to the lead plates oxygen is released from the positive plates. The oxygen mixes with hydrogen in the electrolyte to form water. As this reaction continues the acid becomes weaker and weaker, and more and more sulfate coats the plates. Charging the battery reverses the chemical process, forcing sulfates back into solution with the electrolyte and causing oxygen from the solution to move back onto the positive plate.

The down side to all this charging and discharging business is the inevitable flaking of lead particles off the plates until the battery's ability to act as a battery is greatly diminished. Further affecting battery performance is the fact that when a battery is left discharged the sulfates penetrate too deeply into the lead plates and cannot be driven back into solution, creating the condition often referred to as "sulfated."

Specific gravity is often used to check the state of charge for non-sealed batteries. Specific gravity simply measures the weight of a liquid as compared to water. The specific gravity of a fully charged battery (with strongly acidic electrolyte) ranges from 1.260 to 1.280 at 80 degrees Fahrenheit or 1.260 to 1.280 times as heavy as the same volume of water. As the battery becomes discharged the specific gravity drops because the electrolyte has a higher percentage of water. This is also why a discharged battery will freeze on a cold winter's night while a fully charged battery will not.

Low and no-maintenance batteries change the chemical and physical construction of the plates slightly. By adding a chemical like

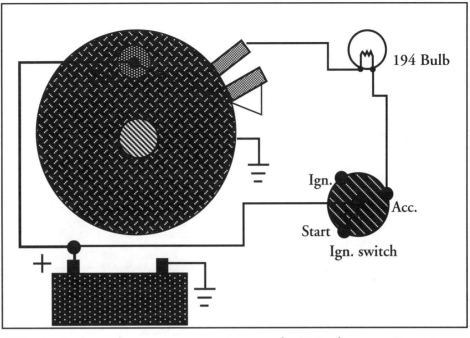

194 Bulb

Ign.
Acc.
Start
Ign. switch

This circuit shows the easiest way to wire an early G.M. alternator. By wiring the exciter wire off the accessory position (instead of the ignition position), you eliminate run-on when the key is shut off caused by voltage fed back from the alternator.

Early-style G.M. solenoids have two small terminals, one is hot only when the starter cranks and is used as a resistor by-pass with points-style ignition circuits.

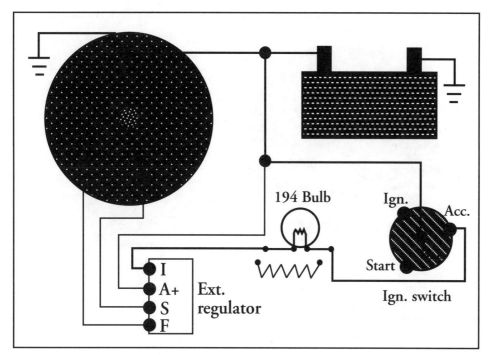

Early Ford alternators use an external regulator. Be sure to use a fusible link where the alternator wire connects to the battery.

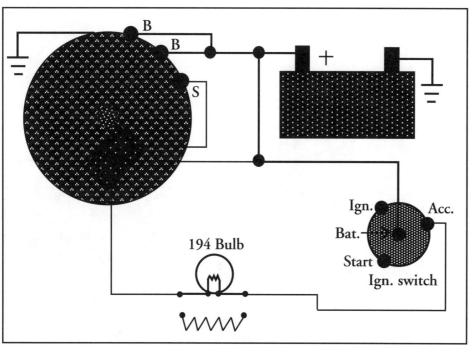

Late model Ford alternators use two B terminals to handle the heavy current loads. Output wire should be at least 8 gauge in any alternator installation - 6 gauge or heavier if the output hits 100 amps or more.

calcium to the plates and changing the structure of the plates themselves, gassing of the battery is greatly reduced. This means a much smaller volume of corrosive/explosive gasses, little or no loss of water, and generally improved performance.

Recombination batteries, sometimes known under the name valve-regulated, go even further. These batteries contain all the "electrolyte" in a porous glass mat positioned between the cells. There is no liquid acid in batteries of this type and they can be mounted in nearly any position. As a General Motors engineer explained, "the chemistry is the same as a conventional lead-acid battery, but the hydrogen and oxygen can move back and forth from the plates to the glass mats without the gassing you see in a standard 'flooded' battery design."

Sometimes confused with recombination batteries, the new gel-cell batteries are quite different internally. Though they are often used for golf carts or stationary applications these designs are currently not suitable for automotive applications because they are so easily damaged during recharging.

Deep cycle batteries

Golf Cart batteries are known as deep-cycle, meaning they are designed to be discharged to less than half their capacity with no ill effects. A standard automotive battery, by contrast, is designed to put out a short burst of high-amperage power, to start the car, and then be quickly recharged by the alternator. Using an automotive battery in a deep cycle application will shorten its life considerably.

Keep it charged for long life

All batteries self discharge to some extent. This means a fully charged battery will draw itself to zero voltage over time, even if the battery cables are removed. The answer is to recharge the battery when the vehicle sits for any extended period. This becomes doubly important with the new fuel injection and radio designs which place a small load (but still a load) on the battery at all times. Don't allow the battery to run down and don't let it sit for any length of time in a discharged condition.

Other tips for long life are mostly common sense. Keep the battery clean because a film of acid and dirt will conduct a small current between the terminals, speeding the self discharge.

Mounting the battery

Batteries, with the exception of the truly sealed recombinant designs, emit gasses that are very corrosive and explosive. When mounting any battery be sure to keep it away from high heat areas like exhaust pipes and manifolds. It's also necessary to keep the battery

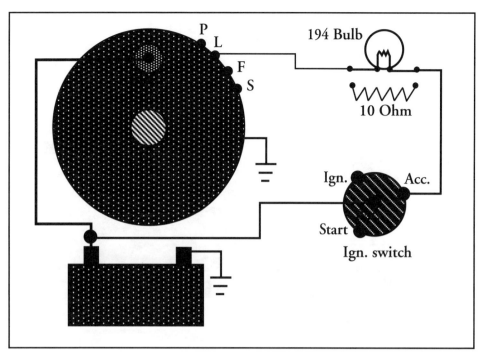

Not a one-wire, late model G.M. alternators (CS series) require two wires to operate. Light in exciter circuit limits amperage and also functions as charge-indicator light. 10 Ohm resistor can be used in place of #194 bulb.

Early and later style Ford alternators use the same size shaft though they may or may not come with the right pulley.

Two G.M. alternators. On the left, an early style alternator with internal regulator. On the right is a small-diameter CS alternator used on late model cars.

This is a late model Ford alternator with new upgraded output wires (some Fords suffer overheated and damaged terminals).

away from any source of sparks, such as the ignition system, that could accidentally ignite the gasses vented by most battery designs.

The closer the battery is to the starter the better it will perform in starting the engine. Different vehicles have larger or smaller areas to mount batteries in and often the battery for a hot rod is mounted in the trunk. In these situations it's good to remember that the farther the battery is from the starter, the larger the battery cables need to be in order to prevent excessive voltage drop. Though it's common practice to use the frame as the main conductor on the ground side of the battery-starter circuit, it's a better idea to run a ground cable from the battery negative post to the engine.

The use of a marine grade battery box to house the battery will protect the trunk from acid spills and also protect the battery case from damage due to items carried in the trunk. Some of the standard batteries use a vent tube, (Delco for example) which can be run through the floor if the battery is mounted in the trunk or interior of the car. Otherwise, the battery box itself must be vented to the outside or the battery must be one of the truly sealed recombinant designs.

Battery cables are heavy so it is important to route the cables in a way that provides them with plenty of support. Running them inside of the frame or solidly attached to the outside of the frame will prevent them from drooping and rubbing on a sharp frame edge or a bracket. The last thing you want is to have the cables wear through their insulation, or come in contact with the drive shaft or the exhaust system. Use plenty of brackets and ties to keep the cable(s) out of danger's way.

When converting from an early to a late style alternator you may have to convert the new unit back to the non-serpentine belt.

STARTERS

Factory starters can be broken down into three basic styles: Those that use a solenoid attached to the starter like most G.M. designs. The bare starter with the solenoid mounted to the fender or firewall, often used by Ford. And the gear reduction starter used by some Chrysler products, which uses both a solenoid attached to the starter and a starter relay.

At the heart of all starters is a powerful electric motor. Most starter motors are made up of two or four field windings inside a heavy steel case. Rotating inside the field windings is the armature, wound with many windings of copper wire. Each armature winding is attached at the copper commutator, where the brushes connect the various windings to the battery and ground as the armature and commutator rotate.

When the starter is energized, current moving through the field windings creates a strong magnetic field with a north and south pole. Current moving through the armature creates a magnetic field in one or two of the windings. This magnetic field in the armature winding is attracted to, or repelled by, the magnetic poles of the field windings. It is this attraction and repulsion of magnetic forces, between the field and armature windings, that causes the armature to turn. As the

This early style Ford alternator must be used with a matching external regulator.

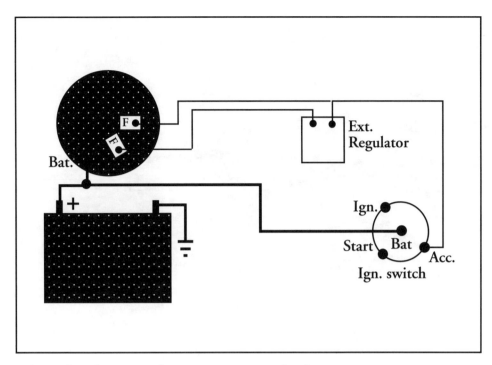

This early style Mopar alternator circuit uses the electronic, not mechanical, voltage regulator.

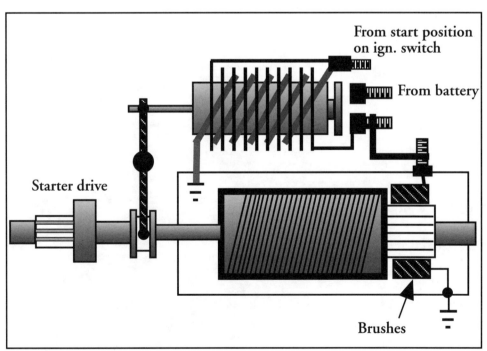

Typical G.M. starter solenoid uses two windings, a pull-in and a hold-in. Both are activated when you first turn the key, though as soon as the drive engages the flywheel the pull-in winding looses its ground and is thus de-activated.

starter turns, different commutator strips line up with the brushes and a new set of windings are energized, putting continual torque on the rotating armature.

Despite the tremendous torque created by most starters, enough to crank over a big block V-8 on a cold morning, some engines require even more. Even without the need for more torque, some applications call for a smaller starter that provides more clearance between the starter and some nearby component like the headers or steering box. In answer to these needs we now have the high torque mini starter.

The high torque mini starter is being used in all types of applications. First designed for racing applications, the mini starter is popular for the hot rod builder because of its small size and extra torque. The size means more clearance around the starter and better air circulation so it is less likely to be affected by heat from the exhaust headers or manifold. The extra torque helps to turn over engines with extra displacement or compression.

When installing a starter, remember that the battery cable needs to be large enough to carry the current without excessive voltage drop, and kept away from the manifold and edges of the frame. The connection between the battery cable and the starter or solenoid must be kept clean and tight. As already mentioned, the starter must have a good ground. In most situations that means the cable from the negative battery post should go directly to the engine block.

STARTER SOLENOIDS

Described briefly in Chapter One, starter solenoids are the switch between the starter and the battery.

Two main types of solenoids are used: the direct mount where the solenoid mounts directly on the starter (G.M. style) and the remote mount, where the solenoid is mounted on the fender well or frame and a cable connects it to the starter (Ford style). Both are good systems, the direct mount solenoids are more likely to encounter hot-start problems due to heat build-up from the exhaust system.

Solenoid failure, or non-operation, is often due to excessive heat. As heat builds up so does resistance. The extra voltage and current required by the solenoid to overcome the resistance is, at times, not available because the battery cables are too small or the connections are dirty and corroded.

A number of devices have been offered over the years to help owners overcome this hot start problem. The most common and useful is the kit made up primarily of a standard 30 amp relay that is located in the starter switch circuit. When the ignition switch is turned to start the relay is activated and in turn transmits power from the battery terminal of the starter directly to the S terminal on the solenoid. This is, in effect, a safe way of shorting the two terminals together with a screwdriver.

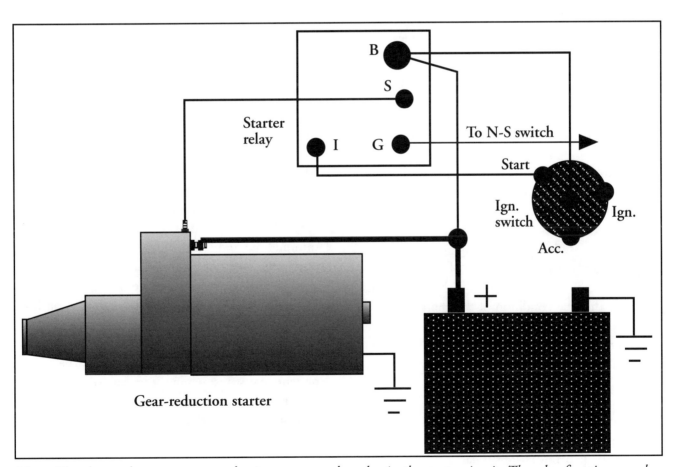

Many Chrysler products use a gear-reduction starter and a relay in the starter circuit. The relay functions much like a "hot start" add-on relay in a G.M. starter circuit. Terminals on the relay do not always have the designations shown.

CHARGING SYSTEMS

The battery provides energy to start the car. Once it does start that energy must, of course, be replaced. The charging system is designed to bring the battery back to a state of full charge and provide the power needed to run all the electrical systems on the vehicle.

Two different types of charging systems have been used in automobiles. Up until about 1960 most cars used a generator while from that point on most cars relied on an alternator to keep the battery charged and provide energy for the vehicle electrical system.

A generator produces direct current voltage (DC) and uses a regulator to control the current and voltage output, and to connect the generator to the battery.

Alternators produce alternating current, (AC), in which electrons flow first in one direction and then in the other. Since DC is used in automobiles, the AC current coming out of a raw alternator must be converted to DC. Diodes, often mounted in the alternator frame, convert the AC to DC electricity. Unlike generators, alternator current output is self regulating. Voltage, however, must be regulated. Though the first alternators used an external regulator for voltage, most alternators used on late model automobiles use an internal voltage regulator.

Note: All alternator systems sense system voltage in order to determine the correct voltage output of the alternator. Thus a bad battery will make it impossible for the alternator to work correctly and may also make testing of the alternator difficult. Because it's so important that the regulator sense the true condition of the charging system, it's very important that the alternator or generator and any external regulator be well grounded. If in doubt use a star washer under the regulator base or a separate ground wire.

CONSTRUCTION DETAILS
Generators

DC generators are similar to starter motors in construction. The housing contains two field coils which create a magnetic field. Rotating inside the field coils is the armature wound with many windings. As these armature windings cut through the magnetic field created by the field windings a voltage is induced in the armature winding and fed to the commutator and then on to the brushes.

Because the field wires of a generator are wrapped around a permanent magnet, there is always some magnetic field for the armature windings to cut through. This is why you can push start an old car with a dead battery - the generator in the old '54 Chevy, with its permanent magnets, will "self excite" once it starts to turn. With a modern car, however, there must be some battery voltage before the alternator will produce energy.

Generators require a regulator to control current and voltage output. Most generator regulators are mechanical in design and use three sets of points, controlled by three corresponding coils of wire, to control voltage, current and the connection between the generator and the battery.

Generators have a number of disadvantages when compared to alternators. Not only do they suffer generally lower total outputs, they need more RPM to produce power. If that weren't enough, generator brushes tend to wear relatively quickly as they ride on the segmented commutator.

Alternators

Alternators were first used in mass produced automobiles in the early 1960s and have evolved into very sophisticated devices requiring minimal maintenance while producing power outputs undreamed of by generator designers.

Alternators contain the same basic components seen inside a generator, though the components are essentially reversed in position when compared to a generator. That is, the field windings are actually contained in the rotor, the component that spins; while the stator (which takes the place of the armature) is stationary and mounted to the alternator case. Because alternators produce alternating current (AC), two banks of diodes are used to convert this to direct current (DC).

Detroit switched from generators to alternators for good reason. Most alternators produce more power than a generator, and are able to provide a high percentage of that power at a relatively low speed. In addition, alternators will more readily spin to high rpm without damage. And though both generators and alternators contain brushes, the small alternator brushes run on the smooth slip rings of the rotor and thus last for a very long time.

Because factory alternators don't have a permanent magnet as part of their field windings, they will not self-excite. That is, no matter how fast you spin an alternator it will not produce power until the field is energized by an outside voltage source.

By adding permanent magnets, however, to a G.M. alternator some aftermarket companies have created the "one wire" alternator. Because these units are internally regulated they need only one wire, the output wire which typically runs to the battery. The "one wire" alternator has become very popular with hot rodders due to the ease of installation. The main disadvantage to these alternators is that a dash warning light may not be wired in and the use of a voltmeter or ammeter will be required. Also, most of these are based on earlier G.M. alternator designs so total output is not as high as the more modern alternators.

Note: the large wire

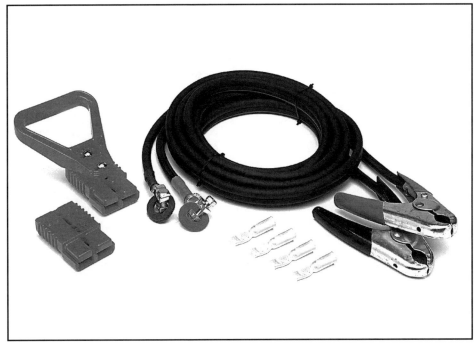

This system permanently mounts a high-quality connector to your car or truck for easy jump starts. Great for hidden battery locations. Painless Wiring

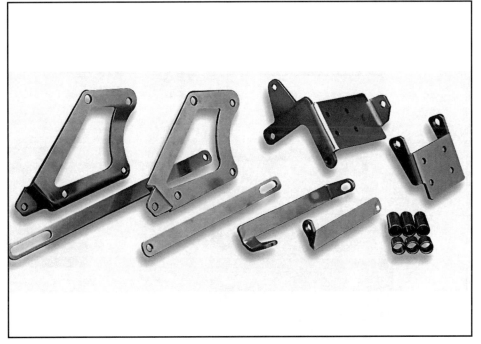

Small block Ford engines can run A/C, alternator and power steering pump with these steel brackets from Painless. Designed for serpentine belt and reverse-rotation water pump.

on the back of any alternator is hot all the time, thus many factory installations include a insulating cap of some type where the wire attaches to the alternator. Also note the output wire needs to be sized large enough to carry the full output of the alternator. In most cases this means *at least* an eight gauge wire.

HOW TO CHOOSE AN ALTERNATOR

One question that often comes up when building a car is: "How big an alternator do I need?"

In answer, remember that bigger is not always better. An alternator rated at 100 amps output will seldom put out more current than one rated at 65 amps. The output ratings are in direct relationship to the engine rpm. The larger, in size and output, alternators normally only have maxi-

mum outputs at their maximum rated rpm range.

When choosing an alternator, determine first the amount of current needed by the system during full load conditions. The size of the alternator you choose should be close to that amount. Remember that it is very rare that all the circuits in the vehicle will be turned on at one time.

Plenty of hot rods are equipped with General Motors alternators simply because the drive train is likewise based on G.M. components. Among the newer G.M. alternators is the CS model, used on many G.M. products starting in about 1987. Smaller than the earlier alternators, these units are readily available in the junk yard or at swap meets and come in outputs as high as 140 amps and sometimes more.

This alternator offers a number of advantages for a prospective street rodder looking to

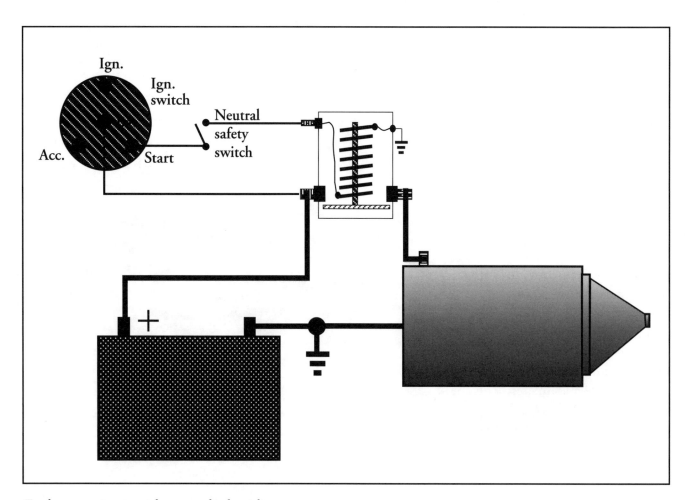

Ford starter circuit with external solenoid.

40

replace an earlier style G.M. alternator or simply install a late model alternator.

The shaft size is the same as earlier alternators, which means you can install either a V-belt or serpentine pulley. The mounting lugs are very similar to earlier alternators, which makes upgrades relatively easy. And wiring is a fairly straight forward proposition.

Charging system wiring

The wires for the charging system are as important as any wires in the vehicle. The main concern is the feed wire from the output post of the alternator to the battery. This wire must be capable of carrying the maximum output of the alternator, which may be 80 or 100 amps. Many times this wire is too small, a gauge size that won't handle the heavy current load and may become very hot or melt during full load operation. If you check the IASCA charts, a 50 amp circuit that's four feet long requires an 8 gauge wire, and 50 amps is minimal alternator output these days. In addition, use a fusible link where the alternator connects to the battery or battery power. When working near the alternator output terminal remember that the terminal is hot all the time. A wrench laid between the terminal and the engine quickly turns into an arc welder.

Alternator exciter wires are usually small in gauge size because they are only transmitting a signal to the regulator, telling it when to charge and how much. They should, however, be at least 16 gauge to prevent too much voltage drop. Most systems require a small bulb or a resistor in the circuit between the switch and the alternator (see the diagrams in this chapter for more on alternator wiring).

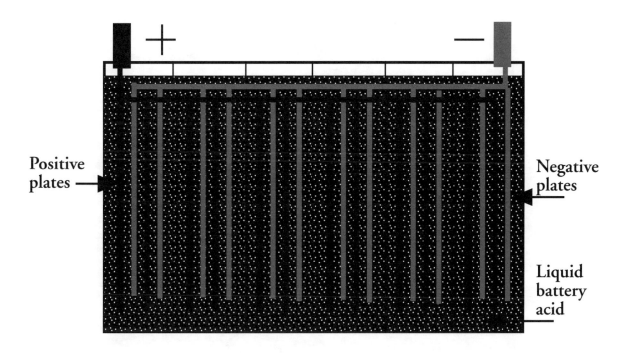

Positive plates

Negative plates

Liquid battery acid

Typical wet-cell batteries group alternating negative and positive plates in 6 cells, each capable of producing 2 volts.

Chapter Three

Switches

Turn it on, turn it up

Switches allow us to turn the power off and on in the various circuits. The topic might seem almost too simple. Yet, consider that in addition to factory switches for everything from headlights to heater fans, the aftermarket offers similar switches in "universal" styles, plus heavy duty and waterproof models.

CHOOSING THE RIGHT ONE

Switches need to be evaluated in terms of

The switch you install should be matched to the need - both in terms of physical fit and style, and of course the current carrying capacity.

the job they have to do. Before buying a switch to serve a particular function, consider the following:

1. Will the switch physically fit in the desired location?

   If you have a round hole in the dash, obviously you would want a round mounting stem style switch. You need to ensure that there will be enough clearance behind the dash so the terminals won't short out against a support or another component located behind the dash.

2. Does the switch have enough current carrying capacity?

   Overloading the switch is probably the most common cause of switch failure. All switches are rated for voltage and amperage maximums. In circuits where there is a large load, such as an electric fan or fuel pump, the amperage draw is greatest at start up and often overloads the switch. By using a relay you can reduce the load on the switch and thus prevent the failure. (See Chapter Five for more on relay kits and their installation).

3. Will the switch have enough internal circuits?

   A single switch may control one circuit or many circuits. The internal workings of switches determine their usage. The use of a toggle switch to operate the lighting system of a car would not be a good idea because the switch does not have enough internal circuits.

4. Will the switch have the proper hookups for the wiring?

   Along with internal circuits, output terminals on the switch must match the needs of the operating device. A light switch is a good example. As mentioned earlier, a light switch has several internal circuits and will have several output terminals to transmit power. If a toggle switch were used for the same job, several wires would be required on a single terminal which presents a real problem.

Factory-style headlight switches are available from many sources, just be sure they come with the knob. Painless Wiring sells a factory switch with knob and the wiring plug.

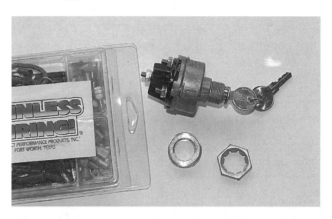

Universal ignition switches are designed to use bayonet or ring terminals. These simple switches offer Start, Ignition and Accessory terminals.

Universal headlight switches like this use screw-on bayonet terminals. Note the circuit breaker integrated into the switch at the back.

TYPES OF SWITCHES
Light switches

Light switches come in many different configurations. The most popular switch being used is the G.M. style. This switch has two internal circuits, one for headlights and one for the running lights. This separate internal circuitry allows for two battery inputs for safety. The double battery feed means that if one circuit fails the other circuit will allow the vehicle to maintain some type of lighting.

This switch has provisions for parking lights, taillights, dome lights, headlights and a dimmer control for the dash lights.

The universal style of light switch, unlike the G.M. style, has only one power input which may be protected by a fuse or a circuit breaker built into the switch. These switches have individual circuits for headlights, tail lights, parking lights and a dash light dimmer control. Compared to a factory switch, these switches are more compact but also offer fewer features.

Toggle or push-pull switches may also be used as a light switch, though the internal circuits will be limited to one or two.

Headlight dimmer switches

A dimmer switch is used to direct current to one circuit or another. With a typical headlight circuit, power comes in from the headlight switch and the dimmer directs output current to the high or the low beam lights. There is no off position on a dimmer switch. If power is supplied the switch simply redirects it to one circuit or the other. Dimmer switches may be floor mounted or steering column mounted, though most have the same terminal configuration and perform the same function.

Some late model, column mounted switches, also provide for flashing the high beams during daylight hours as a passing signal. This provision does require a constant hot circuit (one that does not come through the headlight switch), usually the same circuit as the headlights are on from the fuse block.

Ignition switches

As with other circuits, the ignition and starter circuits require specialized switching. The two main styles are the in-dash universal switch and the column mounted switch.

The in-dash switch is used most often when the column is designed to be straight and smooth. Vehicles built before 1969 and even some later models, had the switch in the dash or console. Some very early model vehicles used a simple off and on ignition switch with the starter activated either by a second, floor-mounted or dash-mounted push button.

Overloading the switch is probably the most common cause of switch failure

---

The in-dash switches of today have ignition, start and accessory circuits built in. Universal ignition switches have screw terminals while factory style switches have spade connectors in a molded housing designed to accept a plug in connector.

The only disadvantage to the modern ignition switch (especially the aftermarket style) is the amount of current it can safely handle. Some of our modern creature comforts require current draws high enough to overload the switch. The use of power relays on circuits such as air conditioning and electric fans will help prevent overloading.

Of the two styles of ignition switch the column mount is becoming the switch of choice. With only a few exceptions, all steering columns built after 1968, had the key and ignition switch mounted on the column. On these columns the switch itself is actually mounted at the base of the column. A control rod connects the switch with the keyed cylinder. The position of these switches is adjustable in case the key position is off slightly.

Different manufacturers design the internal workings of their switches differently. The most commonly used columns and switches are the G.M. (Saginaw) and Ford. Both switches are equipped with multiple internal circuits and can carry large amounts of current. The main difference is in the starting circuits. G.M. starters use a solenoid that requires a lot of current to activate, so their ignition switch has a heavy duty starting circuit. The Ford starter, however, uses a solenoid that requires only a small amount of current to activate so its starting circuit is smaller and more fragile. When using a G.M. style starter with a Ford switch, a starter relay will be required to maintain the life of the switch.

Factory switches, whether column or dash mounted, will generally handle more current than universal switches. Yet it is always safer to use relays for high current devices or circuits.

AFTERMARKET SWITCHES

Before buying a set of toggle switches for your project vehicle, consider the criteria discussed above. Be sure the switch is a high quality component, not a gyppo, plastic-fantastic item from the Ty-aye-wan company. When in doubt about which switch to buy and use, buy a heavy duty or aircraft switch with more than enough capacity to handle the load.

Avoid the temptation to buy aesthetics over function - small and tiny switches are generally only meant for small and tiny loads.

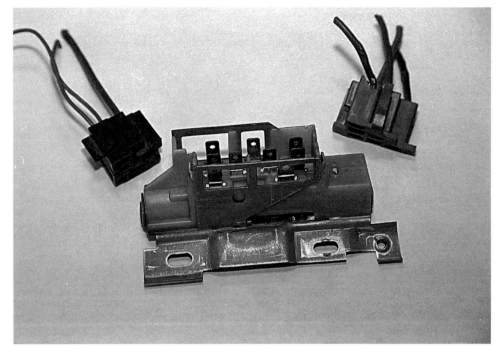

In the flesh, the very common G.M. column-mount ignition switch. Be sure to get the plugs and some wire when you buy that used column.

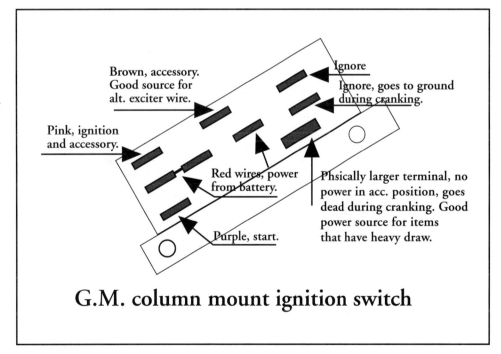

Brown, accessory. Good source for alt. exciter wire.

Ignore

Ignore, goes to ground during cranking.

Pink, ignition and accessory.

Red wires, power from battery.

Phsically larger terminal, no power in acc. position, goes dead during cranking. Good power source for items that have heavy draw.

Purple, start.

G.M. column mount ignition switch

G.M. used this switch from the start of column-mount switches to about 1990. All switches that look like this use the wiring diagram above.

Chapter Four

Gauges

Essential Communication tools

Proper installation of your gauges involves more than just hooking up some wires. Consider that the gauges are the most relied upon source of information in your vehicle. If the gauges are not wired properly the information they present will not be correct.

Proper location is an important factor. Non water-proof gauges would not be suited for engine compartment mounting and gauges not designed for illumination would not be suited for the dash. Use the proper style gauge for a specific application.

Gauges are available in many styles, pick something that works in harmony with the rest of the dash and *interior. Auto Meter*

The most common problem with gauge installations is the lack of a good ground. Since gauges are sensing devices they require only small amounts of current (inputs) to produce their readings. With these small signals the connections are critical.

Proper grounds between the chassis, frame and the body are a must. If when the lights, or any other device, are turned on the gauges read differently, the problem is a bad ground. With the large number of fiberglass parts being used today the issue of grounding becomes even more critical. A ground strap or wire may be needed between the gauges and the body or frame. A good practice is to have a grounding lug located under the dash to help make gauge installation easier.

Outside radio frequencies, noise as it is called in the electronics industry, is another common problem. Impulse signals, such as tachometer and electric speedometer signals, can be interrupted or varied by a magnetic field surrounding a group of wires. For this reason most gauge manufacturers recommend that signal wires to gauges be routed away from the rest of the main harness.

The illumination of gauges is usually simple. Most gauges today come with lights that mount directly into the rear of the gauge housing. The wire pigtail, coming out of the light, goes to the headlight switch. Some styles will have a separate wire for the ground to ensure that it is properly grounded.

Older style and some commercial gauges have small windows around the outside of the gauge housing. These require that small lights be mounted in a bracket and illuminate the gauge face through the windows.

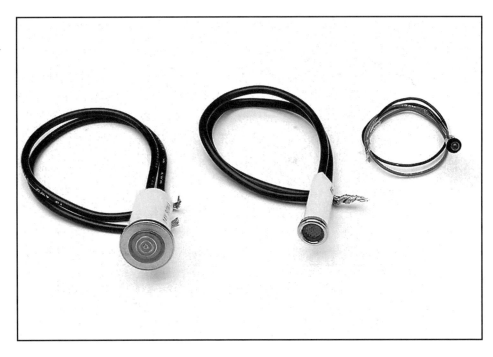

Indicator lights are available in a variety of styles and sizes. Painless Wiring

The best competition tachometers are shock mounted in rubber to minimize impact of vibration.

Painless Wiring makes a gauge wiring harness kit, with connectors for a typical set of gauges and their lights. The wiring kits come with adapters so they will work with either slide-on terminals or round, threaded studs. Brian Montgomery from Painless explains that it's important to use the right sender with a particular gauge. " When people wire and install the gauges they need to be sure the sending unit matches the gauge. Sometimes they try to use a sending unit that's designed for a light with a gauge and the values are totally wrong."

INDICATOR LIGHTS

Indicator lights for turn signals, high beam and many other circuits, are necessary to keep track of vehicle functions. These lights come in a variety of sizes and colors to fit any need. Most of these lights are wired in a common way, with one wire that runs to the proper power source and the other to ground.

Fiber optics is another type light emitting device that is used in some applications. Fiber optics work by transmitting light through a small strand of plastic type material. When light is focused on one end of the strand, the light flows through and is emitted out the other end. The light source is usually a light or bank of lights like normal indicators that are in a remote location. The other end of the fiber can be located wherever the light is needed. Some gauges use fiber optic lights for illumination.

AMMETER OR VOLTMETER?

In the early days of hot rodding the cool cars all ran a group of stand-alone gauges mounted in their chrome plated bracket below the dash. One of those gauges was the ammeter, showing a positive or negative flow of energy to or from the battery.

In more recent years the ammeter has fallen from favor, replaced by a voltmeter. Men and women building a car often ask which is better, an ammeter of a voltmeter? If they don't understand, they sometimes install one and try to hook it up like the other.

First, a few definitions: An ammeter measures current flow (amps) and is installed in series. In a typical automotive application all the current needed to run the car, including all the accessories, goes through the ammeter. That means you have two large, eight or ten gauge, wires up under the dash going to and from the ammeter. A voltmeter, on the other hand, measures the voltage in a circuit and is wired in parallel. That is, the current necessary to run the car and its accessories does not move through the voltmeter. You simply need a light wire to a source of battery voltage and another to a good ground.

Jumping tachometers are usually caused by solid-core plug wires

---

Dave McNurlen at Painless is a big believer in voltmeters as opposed to ammeters. "Voltmeters are safer," explains Dave. " You don't have those big wires running through the dash. Voltmeters are more modern, they still give a good indication of whether or not the charging circuit is working and they're easier to hook up."

"And there's another problem people never consider, a lot of ammeters get overloaded. Because most of those gauges only go to 40 or 50 amps, while the new alternators put out 80 to 100 amps, some go even higher. Old amp meters can't handle the amperage, and if the ammeter overloads and quits so will the car. The old cars that ran ammeters only had a 30 amp charging circuit. The cars had no power windows and no air conditioning, but that's not the case anymore. When people ask me which one to install, I always tell them to hook up a voltmeter."

AVOIDING TROUBLE

For some specialized input, as to the best way to install a set of gauges and avoid any electrical gremlins, we contacted the folks at Auto Meter gauges.

They report that most gauge troubles can be eliminated (hopefully before they start) by paying attention to detail as you wire the gauges. When they get a caller on the tech line complaining that the new Auto Meter tachometer is jumping all over the place, they can usually diagnose it over the phone. Jumping tachometers are usually caused by solid-core plug wires, which produce a great deal of RF noise which in turn affects the tachometer. To correctly wire the tachometer, the green wire should be connected to the negative side of the coil (on a standard ignition), or the Tach terminal on many electronic ignitions. Connecting to the coil terminal on an MSD ignition will damage the tachometer. When in doubt read the directions or contact the gauge manufacturer.

The other common problem, with any of the gauges, is caused by poor grounds. If in doubt about the quality of the ground, Auto Meter recommends running a wire all the way back to the negative battery post.

And though this is a wiring book, the good people at Auto Meter recommend using anti-seize on the threads of the fitting and sender for the mechanical gauges. With anti-seize on the threads there won't be any oxidation between the sender and the block or fitting to affect the readings, and you can take the sender out in a year or two without damaging the sensitive capillary tube.

When trying to decide between mechanical

Complete gauge clusters are available in a host of configurations to fit many street rods and other vehicles. Auto Meter

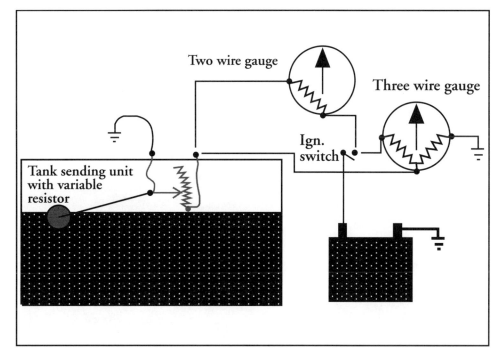

Not all gas gauges are the same. Though two-wire gauges are seldom used any more, the internal wiring of the three-wire gauges is not always the same. All this means you must match the gauge with the sender.

Typical gauges come with either screw-on or spade type connectors. These Stewart Warner gauges (part of the Model A project seen in chapter 9) are being converted from screw-on to spade type.

These gauges, each with its own mount, provide maximum flexibility in mounting position and location. Auto Meter

and electrical gauges, remember that while mechanical gauges are slightly more accurate, electrical gauges make installation easier by using wires instead of capillary tubing. Mechanical gauges do offer a full-sweep dial face for easier viewing of precise measurements.

Another set of problems is caused by sending unit wires and capillary tubes routed too close to header pipes and other sources of heat. Neatness counts, so does common sense. The sender, for example, on a water temperature gauge must actually reach down into the water jacket to get an accurate reading. It can't be mounted away from the block in a T fitting designed to house both the gauge sender and the sender for a light.

Note: Most gauge manufacturers recommend against using sealer or Teflon tape on the threads of an electrical sending unit for fear of eliminating the circuit to ground. However, there are those real-world situations that require a little Permatex Number Two or plastic tape on the threads to eliminate a leak, and in most cases the threads of the sending unit will bite through the sealer to make a good ground.

The Auto Meter technicians note that gas gauges are not all the same, and all factory sending units do not provide the same "reading" to the gauge. Most G.M. gauges read 0 ohms when empty and 90 ohms when the tank is full. Ford and many Chrysler products provide an almost opposite set of readings: 73 ohms when empty and 8 to 12 ohms when full. Some cars read 240 ohms when empty and 33 full. When in doubt, use your ohm meter, connected between the sending unit connection (the one that runs to the gauge) and ground. Now take a reading with the tank empty and full and then refer back to the instructions that came with the gauge to determine if the sender is compatible with the gauge.

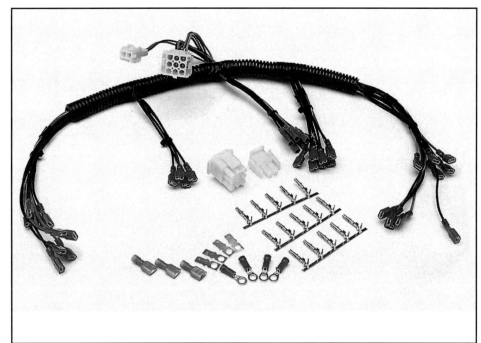

Mounting and wiring the gauges is made much easier with this gauge wiring-harness. Available for both mechanical and electrical speedometers.

Speedometers

With regard to speedometers, those from Auto Meter and most others use standardized fittings and drive cables. If the speedometer is off, correcting it might not be as simple as installing a new driven gear. To obtain correct gear fitment you may have to change both the drive and driven gears. Sometimes a correcting ratio drive joint can be used to adjust the speedometer input. These correcting ratio drives are available from a variety of specialty speedometer shops.

With any gauge, the key to accurate readings is proper installation. Take the extra time necessary for a neat installation and you will be rewarded with proper operation.

The Model A (Chapter 9) uses Stewart Warner, Wings, gauges. These include an electric speedometer, "driven" by a reluctor that screws into the speedometer drive unit on the transmission.

Chapter Five

Wiring the Accessories

Add circuits the right way

This chapter is about wiring electrical accessories, which often involves adding extra circuits. Whether you're adding circuits to an existing harness to run the power windows, or looking for information on air conditioning cir-cuits, we've tried to provide some basic wiring guidelines and in some cases, a few typical dia-grams. There is also material in this chapter that didn't fit anywhere else, like the information about electric cooling fans and a discussion of

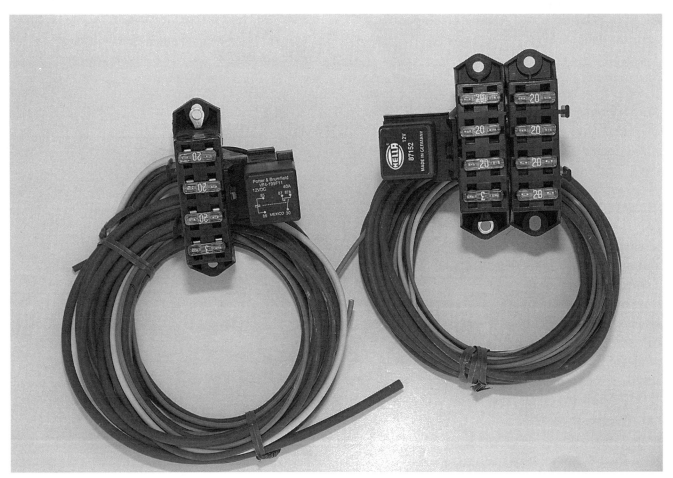

A variety of products are available to help you safely add accessory circuits to your car or truck, including these 3 and 7 circuit CirKit Boss auxiliary fuse pan-els from Painless Wiring. Both offer additional con-stant-hot and ignition-on circuits for accessories like lights, stereo and air conditioning.

the torque converter lock-up kits needed for some applications using the 200 and 700/R4 automatic transmission.

ADDING CIRCUITS

Whether you're adding a set of halogen lights to your 4X4, or an electric fan to the old Chevrolet, there comes a point when you can no longer run the power through the fuse box. Even if the fuse box in question offers extra unused circuits (which many do not), there comes the issue of total current draw moving through the fuse box.

Early style alternators like this from G.M. might not have enough output if you add power-hungry accessories. If you upgrade the alternator be sure the alternator output wire is heavy enough to handle the new load.

The fuse box in your car or truck can only handle so much current without suffering melt down. When it comes time to add a circuit for the new accessory, why not just go ahead and install a second, auxiliary fuse block.

By adding a second fuse block you isolate the new circuits and their current loads from the main fuse block. You're not asking the main fuse block to carry too much current or tagging too many new devices onto existing circuits.

When adding a second fuse block be sure it offers enough circuits to provide for current and future accessories. Decide ahead of time whether you want these circuits hot all the time or only when the ignition is on. Be sure all circuits are protected by individual fuses and that the fuse block has enough total capacity to handle all your present and future accessory needs.

Painless Wiring manufactures a series of fuse blocks that feature both constant-on and ignition-on circuits. The ignition-on circuits use a relay to turn the power on and off. An ignition-on wire is used to power the control side of the relay. When the ignition is turned on the 30

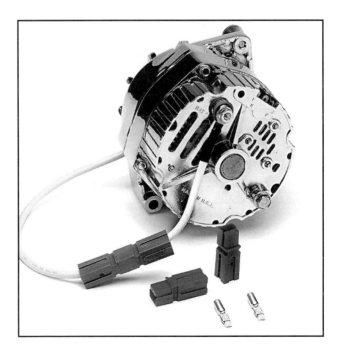

This quick-disconnect kit for the alternator helps to simplify engine swaps. Painless Wiring

amp relay closes, providing power for up to four circuits. A circuit breaker in the main feed circuit protects the fuse block . Each individual circuit is rated at a maximum of 20 amps.

Caution should be taken when adding accessories to your vehicle to ensure the fuse block, fuses and wiring are all heavy enough to carry the load required. Accessories such as power windows and door locks do not normally require a lot of current but when adding a stereo and amplifier the power requirements increase drastically. In some cases the power requirements are so great that power is taken directly from the battery through a large circuit breaker or maxi fuse. (see Chapter Six for more on stereo and stereo wiring). Please consult the operating/owners manual for any accessory that you will be adding to ensure it is provided with the proper power supply.

TRANSMISSION LOCK UP KIT

The 200 and 700R4 Transmission from General Motors requires electronic control of the torque converter. Most of these transmissions are factory installed in cars with computer controlled fuel injection and ignition. That same computer provides a signal to the torque converter, telling it to lock up in third or forth gear, under light and medium load, when the car is moving. If you push the pedal to the floor or apply the brakes, the torque converter reverts to non-lock-up status.

The "black box" control unit provided by Painless and some other aftermarket suppliers takes

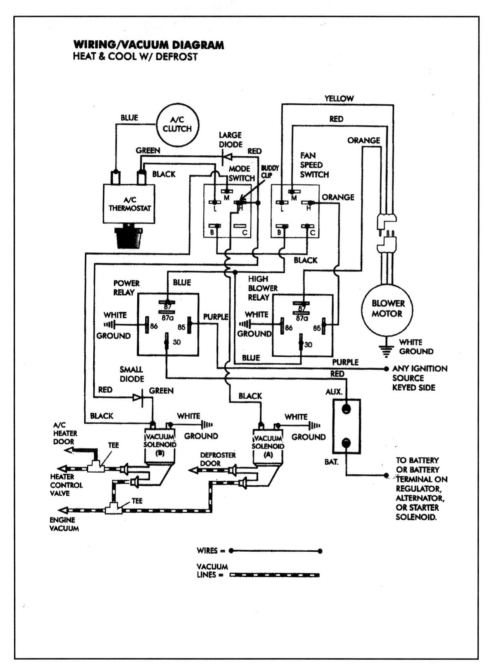

This Heat & Cool wiring diagram from Vintage Air shows how they use two relays to handle the lead to the blower fan (there is no provision here for an electric fan). Note the circuit breaker used on the main feed wire.

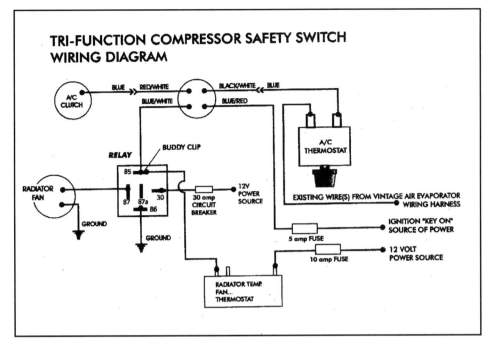

TRI-FUNCTION COMPRESSOR SAFETY SWITCH WIRING DIAGRAM

The three-way high-side switch from Vintage Air is designed to shut off power to the compressor if the pressure is very low, turn on the cooling fan when the pressure hits a pre-determined point and turn off power to the compressor if the pressure goes too high.

the place of the computer input for the 200 and 700/R4 transmission. The kit provides for input to the torque converter so it only locks up in forth gear (most kits don't provide for third gear lock up) under light to medium throttle with no brake application.

When you buy and install a converter lock up kit be sure there is a provision to unlock the converter when the brakes are applied (usually with a brake switch that's separate from the brake light switch). A simple toggle switch to lock and unlock the converter can be extremely dangerous in an emergency situation where there simply is not enough time to remember to turn off the lock-up switch.

AIR CONDITIONING CIRCUITS

For some insight into the unique wiring requirements needed for an air conditioning installation we contacted Jack Chisenhall, owner of Vintage Air in San Antonio, Texas. Jacks sells air conditioning kits for everything from '87

Chevy pickup trucks to '32 Fords, and began the discussion by pointing out the major differences between the various types of cars.

"You need to make a distinction between the way you would approach the air conditioning wiring for a later model car like a '55 Chevy or a Muscle car, and a scratch built hot rod type vehicle.

"Most OEM harnesses for those cars from the 50s and 60s simply

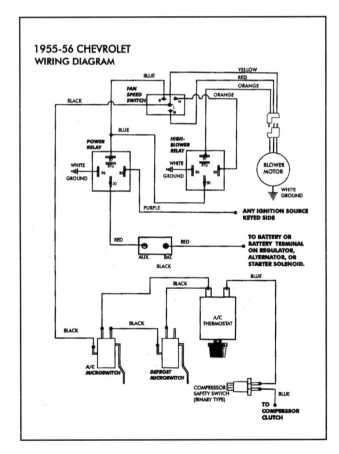

1955-56 CHEVROLET WIRING DIAGRAM

This is a relatively simple A/C circuit, again without any electric cooling fan provision. All power to the fan moves through either the power relay or the high-blower relay. Vintage Air

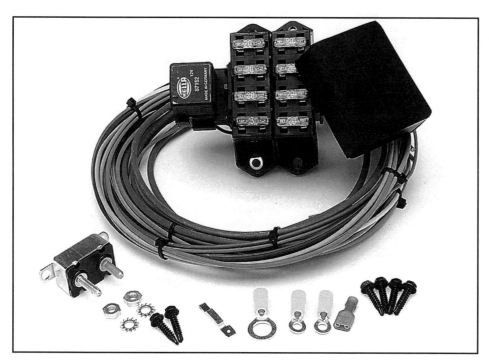

Use this weather resistant auxiliary fuse block for off-road use or situations where the fuse block needs to be mounted in an exposed location.

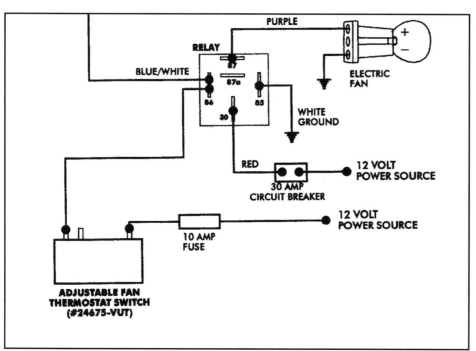

This diagram shows a basic cooling fan circuit, the blue/white wire goes to the high-side switch. In this application the cooling fan is triggered by either the cooling system sensor or the high side switch. Vintage Air

don't have enough capacity to draw the power for the air conditioning through the fuse block. We have a kit that consists of a relay and two circuit breakers, that way we aren't drawing the current from the factory fuse block. We only use one existing circuit to turn on or excite the relay when the ignition is turned on.

"With a scratch built car that doesn't use an OEM style harness, how you power the air conditioning depends on the situation and how much capacity the wiring harness has. Some of the harnesses are designed to accommodate air conditioning."

Discussion of air conditioning wiring always brings up the subject of cooling fans (look for more information on cooling fans farther along in this chapter). More and more hot rodders are turning to electric cooling fans in place of the engine driven fan. "Some of those electric fans just aren't good enough," explains Jack. "They will cool a motor just fine, but they won't provide enough air flow to properly remove heat from the radiator and the air conditioning condenser."

The other mistake people make is to install an electric fan in an air conditioned car and control the fan solely with the engine temperature sensor. To quote Jack again, "By the time that engine is hot enough to turn on the cooling fan, the air conditioning is probably having a problem, the high side pressure is probably already way too high."

More and more of the air conditioning kits that ship from the Vintage Air plant include a three-way switch located in the system's high pressure side. This switch protects the system against very high or low pressure and also turns on the electric fan when pressure on the high side of the system hits a pre-determined figure (more on these switches farther along in the chapter).

Exactly how you wire the air conditioning will depend on the system you install. Aftermarket kits like those from Vintage Air come with their own wiring diagrams. We do provide a few sample air conditioning wiring schematics, provided by Vintage Air, so you can see how the three way switch, the cooling fan and the air conditioning circuits are wired.

ELECTRIC COOLING FANS AND AIRFLOW
Cooling fans

Part of this material is taken from the Jack Chisenhall/Tim Remus book: How To Air Condition Your Car.

Before jumping into the subject of cooling fans we need to consider the

Relays can be added one at a time with a mounting block and relay like these from Painless.

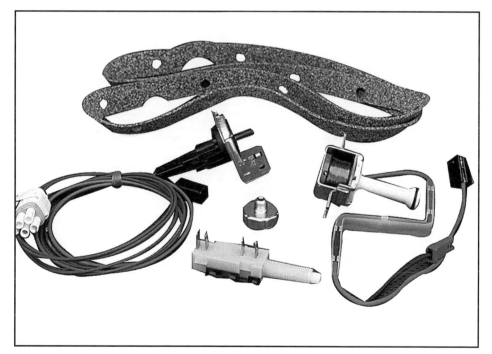

In order to properly run a 200 or 700/R4 transmission in a car or truck without a factory computer you need a conversion kit like this one so the torque converter locks up - and unlocks - at all the right moments.

larger issue of airflow (even if it does seem slightly outside the realm of wiring). An efficient cooling system is only as good as its ability to give up heat to the air moving through the radiator. Some cars (hot rods in particular) have trouble moving enough air over the radiator. The typical V-8 radiator and air conditioning condenser need a *minimum* of 2300 CFM of air moving over it for adequate cooling.

Good airflow is more than just a matter of presenting the full face of the radiator to the air in front of the radiator or grille. The air won't move through the radiator unless the pressure on the back side is lower than the pressure on the front of the radiator. Street rods with smooth sided hoods often provide no good way for the air to exit the engine compartment, no matter what you do with the fan or fans. The final result is a lack of airflow over the radiator and a car that runs hot.

The hood and hood sides need to be part of the overall plan for the vehicle. If the air can't exit the sides of the hood, it must exit below the engine compartment. Sometimes a simple air-dam near the front axle can effectively create a low pressure area behind the radiator and solve an overheating problem by moving more air through the engine compartment.

The fan you use is obviously part of the airflow discussion. The decision is, belt-driven or electric, occasionally both. In a conventional engine layout a good belt-driven fan, operating with a properly designed shroud, will generally move more air than one or two electric fans - all other factors being equal.

A shroud improves the efficiency of a fan (any fan) enormously. Think of it as a funnel, making it possible for the fan to pull more air,

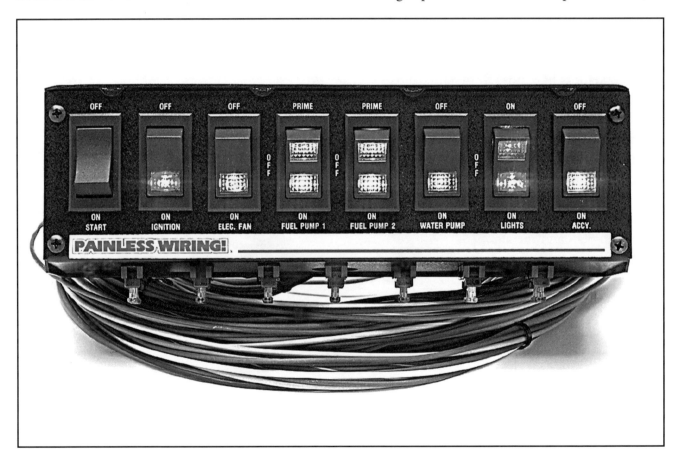

This eight-switch panel uses rocker switches to control ignition, electric fan, 2 fuel pumps, 2 water pumps, lights and one accessory.

more evenly over the entire surface of the radiator. Even a simple "ring" shroud will improve air movement across the radiator and provide a significant improvement in airflow.

Electric fans have the advantage of only coming on when they are specifically needed and drawing no power and no horsepower when they aren't. Though they may not move as much total air as a good belt-driven fan, electric fans will often fit in places much too tight for a good conventional fan.

The first rule of electric fans is: try to pull the air, not push it. Pusher fans, mounted in front of the radiator and condenser, obstruct the airflow all the time, whether they're working or not. The second rule is: always run the fan(s) off a thermostat, not off a manual switch, because it's too easy to forget to turn the fan on in a traffic situation and cook the motor.

The simplest electric fan set ups (in a car without air conditioning) use a thermostat, mounted in the radiator lower tank or the engine, to sense the coolant temperature. When the coolant reaches a certain temperature - meaning it wasn't cooled sufficiently during its pass through the radiator - the sensor turns on the fan. The fan draws air over the radiator and removes heat from the water passing through the radiator. The sensor is typically used to control a relay. Usually the sensor provides the ground for the control side of the relay. Power for the control side can come from an ignition-on or constant-hot power source. The advantage of using a constant-hot power source for the control side is the fact that the cooling fan will run after you

This electric cooling fan from Vintage air comes with its own ring-shroud and adjustable mounting brackets. Note: some fans are designated as pushers, some as pullers.

Vintage Air manufactures temperature sensors, which can be used to turn on the cooling fan, in 2 ranges. Sensor temperature will depend on the system and the thermostat being used.

Painless makes 12 and 18 circuit fuse boxes, other companies may offer more or less. When building a complete car be sure to buy a harness kit/fuse block with enough circuits to handle all your electrical needs.

shut off the car, to help dissipate the heat soak that often occurs after the car or truck is shut off on a hot summer day.

When an electric fan(s) is used on a car with air conditioning, it must be integrated with the air conditioning as well as the cooling system. On a hot day with a cool engine idling and the air conditioning on, the pressure in the high side of the air conditioner can rise very rapidly. The high side pressure can go as high as 400 or 500psi, enough to rupture a hose or blow the hose off the fitting. You need a high side switch that turns on the fan(s) at about 350psi, thus moving fresh air over the condenser and lowering the pressure (temperature and pressure are closely related, as the temperature comes down so does the pressure).

When installing an electric fan, use a temperature sensor that goes into the lower (or cooler) radiator tank (or the engine) and avoid sensors that clamp to the outside of the radiator. An adjustable-temperature sensor is a nice feature.

The high-side switch can be a multi-function switch like that mentioned earlier. The three way switch from Vintage Air has three functions: 1. To act as a high-side fan switch. 2. To function as a high-side cutout, cutting power to the compressor

A good shroud, available in many sizes and shapes, will improve the cooling ability of nearly any fan, belt driven or electric.

clutch if for any reason the pressure goes above 375psi. 3. To act as a low-pressure cutout, cutting power to the compressor clutch when the pressure gets very low, meaning a loss of refrigerant and lubricant as well.

The fan you buy should be the biggest one that will fit your particular application. The blades near the hub of a fan don't move much air - nearly all the work the fan does is done near the tips of the blades. As the blade gets longer, the percentage of blade that is away from the hub increases and the speed of the blade tip increases - making for a fan that can move significantly more air. Some of the newest designs incorporate their own ring-style shroud, a nice feature that will improve the fan's ability to move air.

Jack Chisenhall warns potential fan buyers to use caution when buying fans, as not all cooling fans are created equal. To quote Jack: "Many of the fans simply aren't good enough, they're meant to cool the engine or act as secondary fans. You have to be sure the unit you buy is designed to provide adequate airflow for the engine *and* the air conditioning condenser. You have to know what the capacity of the fan is. Sometimes the only way to be sure you're getting a good enough fan is to buy from a good reputable supplier.

"The best fans have large diameter, broad blades and they have a relatively high wattage rating. Because the amperage draw is significant, a good fan needs a proper circuit. Some of the big ones draw 25 to 30 amps, and 35 amps at start up."

Wiring your fan is just like wiring any other accessory. Use a good switch, if the switch won't handle the load, use a relay.

Electric fans come in various sizes, buy the biggest one you can, ask if the fan has a CFM rating and whether or not it's meant for installation ahead or behind the radiator.

Chapter Six

Automotive Audio

From $89.99 to $8999.99

If you haven't gone shopping for car stereo lately get ready to be overwhelmed. Things have changed. With current components and technology there's almost no limit to the sound available in your car or truck. Whether it's quality, quantity or both that you require, the only limit is your imagination, and of course your wallet.

Systems with 2000 or more watts are as close as your local specialty stereo shop or retailer. After a trip to the stereo store, the system you

Today you can have anything you want in car audio. Be sure to spend time perusing the racks at your local stereo shop before paying out your hard-earned dollars.

were so proud of a few years back might not look much better than the AM radio in Dad's old Buick.

The problem in writing this chapter was knowing when to stop so it remained a Wiring book with a Stereo chapter, not the reverse. The idea here is to provide an introduction to automotive stereo. With that goal in mind we present a brief buyer's guide to help you make sense of the various offerings, a few typical wiring diagrams, and an interview with Kelly Kitzman, a man who's been designing and installing automotive stereo for over ten years.

Also included is a look at one high-end installation. Even if you don't intend to spend 8000.00 dollars putting stereo in your hot rod, there's something to be learned from this installation in a late model Firebird.

WHERE TO START

Current discussions of car audio speak of the "sound stage," or where in the car the music seems to originate. The best systems also provide a good "image" so you can pinpoint the location of each instrument. The quality and location of the front and rear speakers, and how they are angled, all affect the sound stage and the stereo image.

The idea is to make it seem as though Boz Scaggs or the Beach Boys are all lined up on the dash riding to work with you. Better

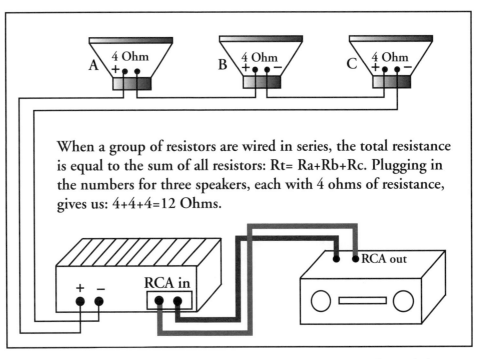

How many speakers you install, and exactly how you wire them, has a major impact on the circuit that the amplifier "sees."

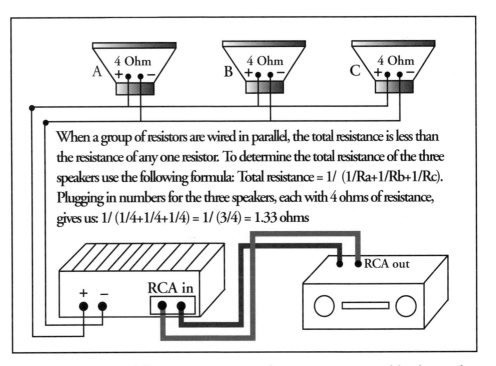

Same components, different wiring. A very low resistance circuit like this might fry your expensive new amplifier - which is why you may need professional help with the design and wiring of your system.

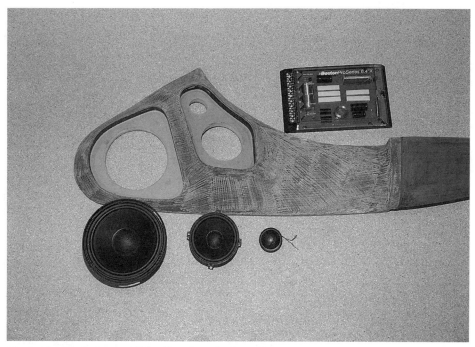

Each Firebird door will be fitted with three Boston Acoustics speakers as shown, mounted in the custom fabricated speaker housing. The cross-over from Boston Acoustics is designed to work with these three speakers.

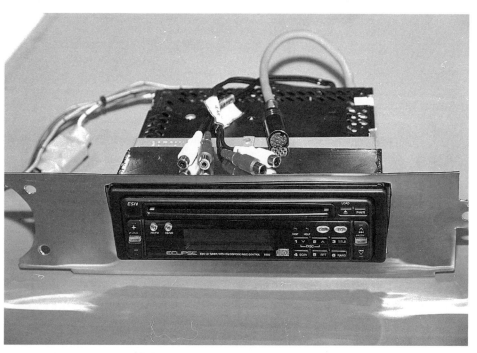

The better quality head units have RCA output cables, used to connect the head unit to an external amplifier(s). This high-quality unit (meant for Kelly's Cadillac) has two sets which allows for more flexibility in system design.

yet, you should be able see exactly where on the stage the lead guitar and the horn section are - all of which makes it tough to keep your mind on traffic and speed limits.

Obviously, you need to start with a good music source, be able to amplify it without introducing any distortion and deliver it to speakers that faithfully reproduce the full musical spectrum. Describing exactly how all this is accomplished (and *whether* it is accomplished) involves the use of a few terms specific to the audio field.

TERMS

Frequency Response: This is the range of frequencies over which a given component can perform. Human hearing runs from about 20Hz (hertz or cycles per second) to nearly 20KHz. Speakers or systems that advertise frequency response to 25 or 30KHz are useful only to your German Shepherd because humans can't hear past 20KHz. In fact, anyone with a little grey in the temples is lucky if they can hear past 10 or 15KHz.

Decibel: often written as dB, is "a unit used to express a relative difference in power of intensity, usually between acoustic or electrical signals, equal to ten times the common logarithm of the ratio of the levels," according to my dictionary. The significant part of the definition is the logarithmic part - which means these measurements are not linear and that twice the power won't get you twice the dBs.

Total Harmonic Distortion (THD): This is a measure of how much the original signal is distorted by a certain component. Obviously, less is better here and the THD numbers can be compared between similar equipment when deciding which to buy.

BUYER'S GUIDE
Head units

Devices that fall under the category, "head unit" include everything from brand-X AM/FM cassette players that cost $69.95 to CD players or AM/FM CD players that cost ten times that much.

Nearly everyone wants an AM/FM radio and most buyers want either a cassette player or CD player. A few of the new units include both a cassette and CD player. You don't have to buy one of these expensive dual units to have both capabilities, however. Many of the new cassette players also offer a "CD controller," meaning an external CD player can be plugged into and controlled from the head unit. Even without this feature a variety of FM-modulated CD players are available that can be interfaced with nearly any AM/FM by bringing the signal in through the antenna lead.

External amplifiers come in various configurations with vastly different power ratings. Note the large gauge power input wires and the way the case is finned to help dissipate heat.

Crossovers come in a variety of shapes and sizes, not to mention price and design. These passive crossovers from B.A. are are designed specifically to interface with the speakers used in the Firebird doors.

A few of the high-end head units have no true amplifier and must be used in conjunction with additional amplifiers. More common among the quality brands are head units that will operate with or without external amplifiers. Without the external amp(s) most head units provide up to 40 watts/channel into four channels (most of these are peak-power specifications). By plugging the "RCA pre-outs" into an external amp the total output can be boosted to hundreds of watts per channel.

Perhaps we should explain that the presence of RCA pre-out cables means the music signal leaves the head unit in "pure" form before it is processed by the unit's internal amplifier. This signal is then amplified by the external amplifier(s) and passed on to the speakers.

The more expensive head units feature two or three sets of pre-out cables so you can use one amp for the front speakers, one for the rear speakers and a third for the subwoofers. Many of these units allow control of the subwoofer from the head unit so you don't need a separate crossover for the fifteen inch speakers on the back shelf.

The high-end head-units offer everything from built in alarms for the whole car, not just the stereo; to radio text - which means they have the ability to display a message broadcast by your favorite radio station along with the music. The better units even include remote control so you don't have to make that long reach to the dashboard.

Before you buy be sure to look at all the options and ask plenty of questions. When you do get out the checkbook buy the head unit that offers the features you want and works best with the rest of the components in your system.

The crossovers are mounted on either side of the car in the cavity where the factory side-speakers once mounted.

Speakers

The best speakers, like everything else, are made up of good components. Most feature relatively large magnets and high quality voice coils. They use speaker cones made from very stiff (yet light) material that won't distort under use. Remember that door speakers are subject to moisture so the relatively inexpensive speakers meant for home stereo applications may not be such a good value.

Speakers are rated in a number of ways. Input sensitivity is the Sound Pressure Level (SPL) the speaker will produce given one watt of power measured at a distance of one meter. When comparing numbers be sure all the specifications were generated using a true one watt/one meter test. Frequency response is simply the range of frequencies the speaker can reproduce within a standard power range. Impedance is the speakers resistance, measured in ohms. As your layout gets more complex, with more and more speakers, you need to keep track of the total impedance or the amplifier can be damaged.

The power handling abilities of the speaker are rated in both nominal and peak values. The nominal rating measures the amount of power the speaker can handle for long periods while peak power measures allowable short term bursts of power.

In terms of what to buy and where to mount them, spend the most money on the front speakers (except for systems that use rear subwoofers). Bass notes represent large sound waves that easily travel over, under and through obstructions to your ear. This means speaker placement is more critical for mid-range and tweeters, whose smaller/shorter sound waves *are* easily stopped by obstructions and thus need a more direct path to your ear.

RCA cables carry the music signal from the head unit to the amplifier, and should be routed to avoid electrical interference from other cables and components.

Rear speakers should be used to provide "fill," and not to dominate the system. Full-range speakers are fine for rear deck applications. In fact, experts say too much treble and high frequency sound coming from the rear speakers confuses the sound stage so expensive tweeters are not what you want behind your head.

Though some new speaker wire looks like welding cable in drag, most speaker installations only require 16 or 18 gauge multi-strand copper wire. Subwoofers, some of which draw as much as a Cadillac starter on a cold morning, will require something closer to those welding cables mentioned earlier.

Amplifiers

A good amplifier will provide enough good, clean power to drive your speakers without adding distortion and without clipping. Clipping

occurs with some amps when they are turned up to "eleven" on the volume dial. Without quite enough power to produce good clean sine waves at high volume, the top of each wave is "clipped off" creating a square wave, which when passed to the speaker is likely to cause melt down.

Specifications used to describe amplifiers include frequency response, continuous and peak-power output. Continuous output usually lists the conditions under which the power was obtained, i.e., 35W/channel into 4 ohms at less than .1% THD. Peak power ratings are often given in similar fashion. As always, be sure you compare apples to apples and that the tests for different units were run under the same conditions (always read the fine print).

The signal to noise ratio refers to the difference between the music output and the "noise"

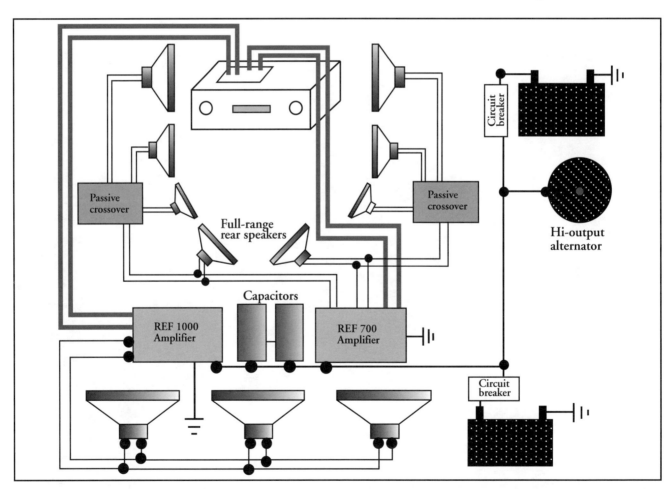

This simplified drawing shows how the various components used in the Firebird are tied together. Note the three subwoofers are wired to one amplifier. Rear fill speakers and the three door speakers are powered from the same amp, though the signal is processed by the crossover before going to the individual door speakers.

that is always present to some degree in any signal. What you want is bigger numbers, more signal and less noise.

Better amps might be listed as "two ohm stable." This means the amplifier can be run continuously with a speaker load of two ohms. As mentioned earlier, multiple speaker set ups can result in rather low overall impedance for each channel. Some amplifiers will overheat when asked to drive low-impedance speakers or speaker combinations. This consideration needs to be figured into your overall system design (see the speaker illustrations on page 63 for a better explanation of how to figure the total resistance of a set of speakers).

How many channels the amplifier should have depends on how many outputs the head unit provides and how many sets of speakers you wish to drive. The better amplifiers provide a number of interesting options in terms of how many channels can be driven and whether or not a central channel or subwoofer can be added. There is no simple formula, you need to design the total system and include the amp(s) as part of that system. Help is available from any good specialty stereo retailer.

Crossovers
Good speakers are specialized, designed to reproduce only a part of the musical spectrum. Woofers are big

The RCA cables hanging out of the dash run to the two external amplifiers. The other wires are used to power the head unit and to trigger the relay that controls power to the amps.

This is the high-end Eclipse head unit used in the Firebird. The head unit can generally be run off the factory radio circuit, though external amps require their own heavy-duty circuit.

69

Under the hood we see a new yellow top Optima battery, a re-wound G.M. alternator and the heavy cable that runs to the two external amplifiers.

and produce big, bass notes. Tweeters are tiny, best used to reproduce cymbals and high frequency notes. A crossover is a filter used between the music source and the woofer, for example, so only the low frequencies will be passed on to that speaker. Likewise a crossover designed to pass only high frequencies can be used to filter out the low frequencies from the signal going to the tweeter.

A crossover can be as simple as the capacitor used between the two speakers in a coaxial speaker set up, or as complex as the dedicated crossover designed to work with certain speaker systems. Passive crossovers like our simple example above have no power supply. Active crossovers, commonly used between the head unit and the amplifier(s), need their own power source.

Some amplifiers have high and low-pass filters, essentially doing the work of a crossover. Again, all this has to be taken into account as you design the system for your vehicle.

HANDS-ON, THE INSTALLATION

The installation shown here is an elaborate stereo system installed in a late model Firebird. With a total of 11 speakers, three of them 15 inch subwoofers, and a total of 1700 watts, this is probably more system than most of us intend to install. Yet it illustrates what a creative person can do

Back side of the custom fabricated speaker panel shows how the plate that holds the tweeter and midrange is tipped toward the driver.

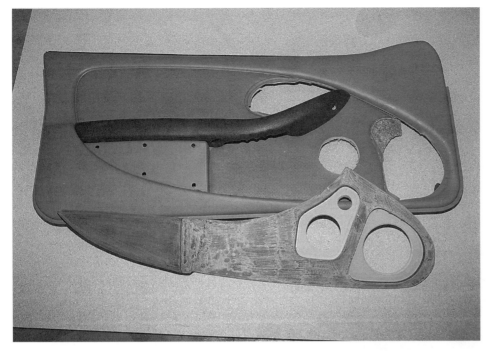

Series set of components, designed specifically to work with these speakers. The "rear" speakers, not to be confused with the massive subwoofers, are 6-1/2 inch co-axial speakers (containing both a woofer and tweeter in one package), also from Boston Acoustics. The deep thumping you can feel in your chest is provided by the three JL 15W6 speakers wired in parallel. No separate crossover is used between the head unit and the

The original door panel, and below it, the custom fabricated speaker enclosure.

with imagination and the best of components. Particularly interesting is the way the custom speaker enclosures are manufactured and covered to match the rest of the car, a trick that can be used in any installation.

The installation is done by Kelly Kitzman at Sound Waves in Fridley, Minnesota.

The components

The components used for this system are among the best available. The head unit is a model 5303 from Eclipse, described as a pre-amp unit (meaning it must be used with additional amplifiers). Kelly installed two additional amplifiers, a REF 700 to drive the front and rear speakers, and a REF 1000 to drive the three big subwoofers.

A passive crossover from Boston Acoustics is used to separate the low, mid and high frequencies before they get to the three individual speakers used in the front doors. Those front door speakers are part of Boston Acoustics' Pro Series. The 6.4 three-way system consists of a separate 6-1/2 inch woofer, 4-1/2 inch mid-range and 1 inch tweeter. The crossover is part of the same Pro-

Kelly holds the large rear speaker enclosure intended for the three 15 inch subwoofers. The box is made from 3/4 inch particle board with fiberglassed corners and a fiberglass floor.

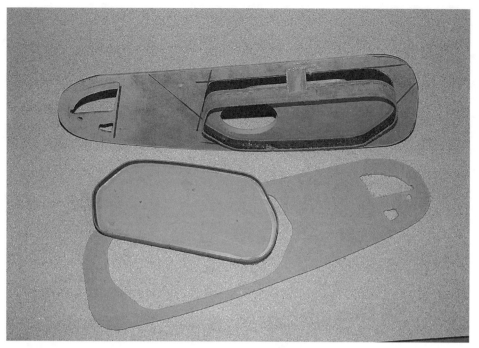

Intended for a different car, the lower half of the photo shows the bare components: the basic panel and the smaller panel that will hold the speaker and aim it at the driver. The upper half of the photo shows the two parts joined together.

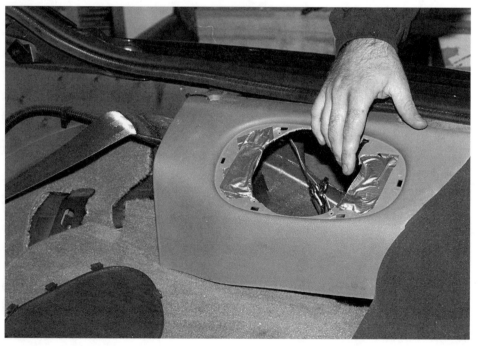

Factory rear speaker holes will be reinforced with particle board and then used to locate the rear "fill" speakers.

amplifier because the head unit provides a separate sub-woofer output which is then fed via RCA pre-out cables to the REF 1000 amplifier.

Other hardware

Kelly installed two "stiffening capacitors" in parallel with both amplifiers. These act as both a buffer, to damp out voltage spikes in the power leads, and as a reserve power source for those instants when the amplifier needs more power than the battery can provide.

Because the amplifier draws up to 200 amps when the system is putting out full volume, the standard alternator and battery just won't cut it. The answer is more twelve volt power for the amplifier. Kelly replaces the standard battery with a yellow-top recombinant design from Optima. To provide enough power for those occasions when the system is playing very loud and perhaps the car is idling through traffic with the air conditioning on, a second battery is added. This second battery is another yellow-top from Optima, mounted in a marine battery case located in the bottom of the large rear speaker enclosure. The second battery is wired in parallel with the main battery and protected by its own fuse.

To keep the two batteries charged the standard G.M. alternator is removed and sent out to a specialty shop where the output is boosted to 180 amps. Kelly explains that, "You can buy aftermarket alternators with 200 amps or more, but they're real expensive, this gets you almost as much power for a lot less money."

Speaker installation

The speakers are arranged in three groups: Three individual speakers will be added to each door, one full-range speaker will be added on either side in the back of the passenger compartment, and three 15 inch woofers will be installed with their own enclosure, at the very back of the car.

Kelly has crafted custom door enclosures for many cars and he makes the whole thing look easy. He learned the basics from a how-to video tape and refined the methods with practice. The process breaks down as follows:

1. Cut out the basic shape of the enclosure from 1/4 inch board.
2. Cut out the sub-sections that will tilt and hold the individual speaker(s).
3. Create short walls around the cut outs with "water board" (a medium weight press-board found at many upholstery shops that can be easily formed when wet).
4. Hot glue the sub-section in the correct position on the basic piece of 1/4 inch board and reinforce it with a small support.
5. Cover the enclosure (not the holes for the speakers) with grille material, covered and spread in such a way that the curves are nice and soft. Other materials could be used here, but speaker grille material works well and its always readily available in the shop.
6. With a brush, spread liquid epoxy resin mixed with catalyst over the cloth.
7. After the resin is dry and the material has some structural strength, cover it with multiple coats of fiberglass mat and more liquid resin.
8. Clean up the edges after the new speaker enclosure has enough strength and is completely dry.
9. Cover with finish material of our choice. Note, by using the correct vinyl a nice factory appearance is achieved.

The first step in covering the door panels is to cut a section that's too big from the correct viny material.

Kelly uses 3M trim adhesive, which he sprays through an inexpensive spray gun.

The trim adhesive is applied to both the vinyl and the speaker enclosures, then allowed to dry before the vinyl is applied.

Applying the vinyl is more than just a glue-and-stick operation. In this case the vinyl came from Pyramid Trim Products in Minneapolis, Minnesota. Vinyl and upholstery supply houses can often match the factory vinyl and trim materials either by using the color and interior codes on the vehicle or by matching a sample from the car to a common factory material they have in stock.

The new fiberglass enclosures must be sanded before applying the vinyl, otherwise the trim adhesive won't stick. After sanding the top of the new enclosures and cutting a piece of vinyl that's a little too big, Kelly sprays liquid 3M trim adhesive (the yellow stuff some of us use to hold gaskets in place during engine assembly) on one of the new enclosures and the back side of the vinyl. After this adhesive dries to the point where it's no longer sticky Kelly begins the application with help from a heat gun. "You should hold your hand behind the material as you heat it with the gun, it's a good way to judge the temperature of the vinyl and the adhesive," explains Kelly. "Your hand should get hot but not too hot. If you hold your hand there so long that it burns your hand, you're going to tear the vinyl because it's too hot. I always do the steepest areas first. In fact you have to be careful when you design the enclosures so you

A heat gun is used to warm the vinyl and make the adhesive sticky again. By holding his hand behind the vinyl Kelly is sure to get the vinyl just hot enough.

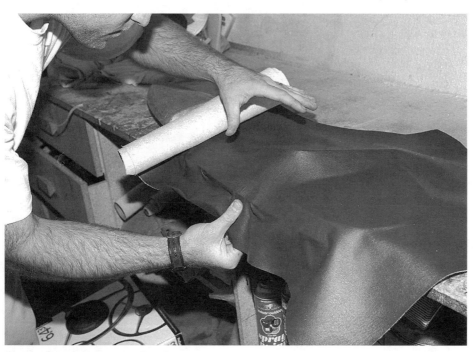

Once the vinyl is hot Kelly stretches it into place, starting on the most curvaceous parts of the door panel.

don't make shapes that are so extreme you can't make the vinyl stretch and stay in place."

Once the vinyl is stuck to the panel, Kelly cuts out the areas where the speaker will mount, leaving enough extra material to roll over the edge and part way down into each recess. Kelly warns that you only want enough extra material to go over the edge and part way down the ridge that surrounds each speaker hole. Extra material that rolls over any of the edges is stapled in place.

Creating the rear speaker enclosure and covering it in vinyl is done in much the same way as the door enclosures, only on a larger, stronger scale. Because the three subwoofers are likely to create enormous sound pressure and vibrations, Kelly builds a very sturdy box and reinforces the top mounting surface with extra layers of fiberglass mat. Covering the top of the rear enclosure is done by following the same steps used for the door skins.

To mount the full-range rear speakers Kelly first reinforces the factory mounting surface with a piece of 1/4 inch board. The board is cut to size and brought in from behind so the speaker mounts to the board and the board mounts to the factory pre-formed panel.

Here you can see how Kelly works across the panel, heating the vinyl, pulling it into position, then heating another section and repeating the process.

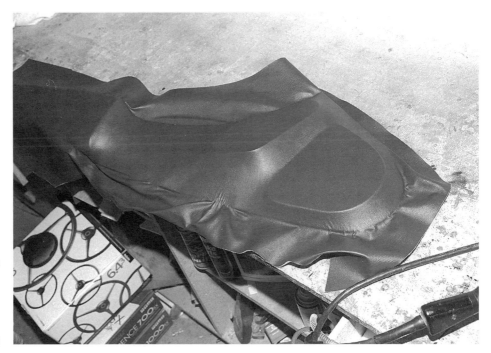

At this point the panel is completely covered, the vinyl is stretched into place.

With a razor blade Kelly cuts out each speaker opening..

Wiring and installation of the head unit, amps and speakers

The head unit is wired to the Firebird's radio circuit. The two amplifiers, however, are wired direct to the car's two batteries through a power relay that is activated whenever the head unit is turned on.

The RCA pre-out cables must be routed carefully so they don't pick up noise from nearby wiring. Kelly runs the RCA cables down one side of the car, and the speaker wires down the same side. The wires you need to keep the RCA cables away from are power wires, thus the power cables that feed the amplifiers are run on the other side of the car. It's also important to keep the RCA cables away from the other circuits the car. Kelly reports that sometimes you can hear a pop in a system whenever the brake is touched, caused by a voltage spike in the brake light circuit being fed to the amplifier through the RCA cable.

In this case, one set of pre-out cables runs from the head unit to the REF 700 amplifier. From there the signal goes to both the full-range speakers used for rear fill, and to the Boston Acoustics crossover. From the crossover the signal moves to the three speakers used in each door.

The other set of pre-out cables runs to the REF 1000 amplifier used for the subwoofers. From the REF 1000 the sub-

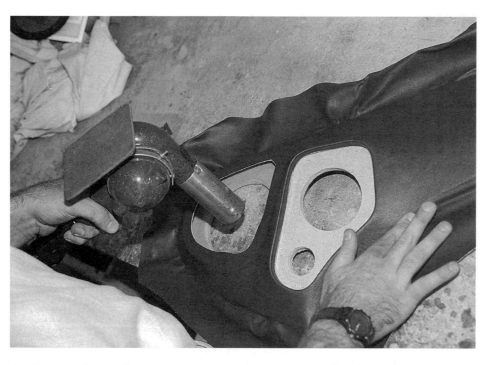

Kelly trims the vinyl so it wraps over the lip at the top of each speaker opening but doesn't extend to the panel at the bottom that mounts the speaker. Heat is used to get the vinyl to adhere and conform to each opening.

76

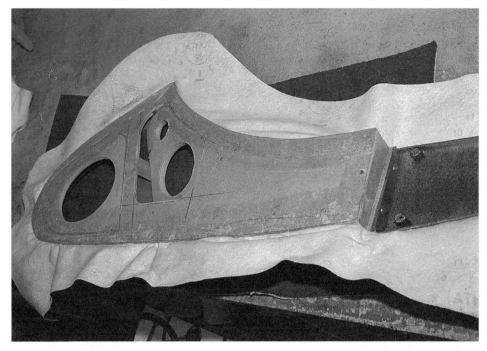

This is the back side of the panel. The final step is to wrap the vinyl around and secure it in place.

a local audio chain store. I worked there for four years and in the four years I was the top installer three of the four years. While I was there I did most of the custom work for the people who were competing at the contests or customers who needed custom enclosures and larger speakers fit into unusual locations. I did that for four years and in 1993 I opened my new company, Sound Waves, with my partner, Tom, who worked at the same big

woofer signal goes direct to the three 15 inch speakers which are wired in parallel.

Interview, Kelly Kitzman at Sound waves
When it comes to high end stereo installations Kelly Kitzman from Sound Waves has seen it all. Whether it's a big Dodge 4X4 or a Ferrari, Kelly has probably installed a stereo system that costs as much as some used cars. Though he does plenty of work for people with substantial bank accounts, Kelly also installs head units and upgrades for individuals with tight budgets, where the dollars must be carefully allocated. Follow along as Kelly explains the principles upon which a good system is based, and how to apply those principles so you get the most sound for your audio dollar.

Kelly, tell me a little bit about yourself and how you learned your trade.

After high school I went into the service and I was stationed in Washington D.C. In 1987 when I was stationed there I started working on car stereos with a friend of mine who worked at a local dealer. I basically worked out of my garage or his driveway for a couple of years. In 1989 I moved back to Minnesota and started working at

Kelly works his way around the perimeter - putting tension on the vinyl and then installing a staple before moving on.

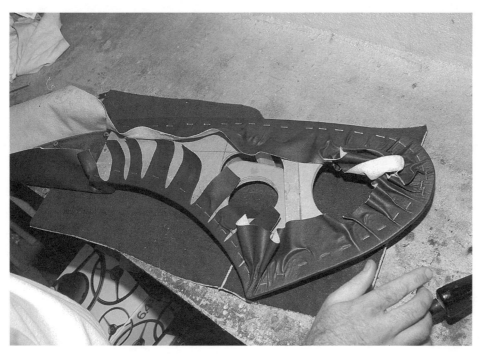

Pie-cuts eliminate the multiple pleats of vinyl and keep it flat on the backside.

After the staples are all in place Kelly trims away the excess vinyl.

chain store I did. In March of 1993 we incorporated the company and opened this store.

Give me a brief description of the kind of work you do. The type of stereo installations.

Our installations run all the way from a $200 head unit to systems that cost $26,000. Some vehicles I work on for 15-20 minutes and others take three months. We try to specialize in customer service, because you have a lot of people who are not familiar with the technology that's out today. They know what they're looking for but don't know where to find it. Or they're just not in touch with what's going on because it changes so fast in this field.

If I'm a customer with a hot rod or maybe an older pickup truck that's fixed up and I don't know what I want for a stereo, how do you guide me through the buying decision?

The first decision you have to make is obviously the money aspect, because that's the big factor. It may not be the first question I ask the customer, but that's the bottom line that needs to be figured out first. The biggest thing is, if you're working on a street rod or a hot rod, you don't want to ruin the integrity of the vehicle. You want your smooth lines; you want it the way *you* want it.

A stereo system can be installed in a vehicle to keep the lines, to keep what you want, to keep the integrity of the vehicle without ruining it. A lot of people don't understand that. You can hide speakers so they're not prominent, or you can customize the locations so nothing is visible.

When the customer comes in, the first thing they're going to be looking for is a radio, obviously. You don't just buy a radio anymore. You have cassette decks, CD players, changers, FM modulated CD changers, five or six different things you can do, so the best thing for a customer to do is to look at a magazine or go to a chain store, and they can see the wide variety of products. You can buy anything you want from a $69 head unit to a $900.00 AM/FM CD player.

So it's kind of like building a car. You have to figure out what you want the car for, what you want the stereo for.

Same thing. Some of the customers just want something to sound real nice. They aren't going to listen to it real loud, but they want it to sound very clean. And then you have customers who want to be heard two miles away.

I should back up here. What is the advantage of buying from a small independent specialty shop like yours as opposed to a chain store.

When you go to a specialty shop you are talking to somebody who knows what they're talking about and is in that field. They don't have to know about

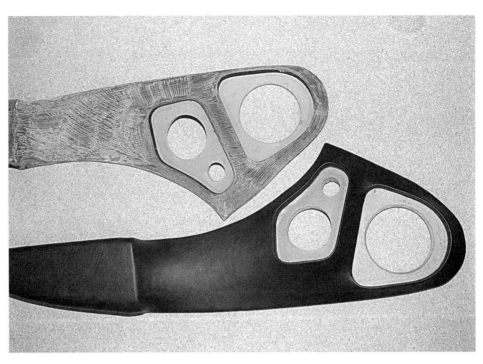

Before and after, one door panel finished and one to go.

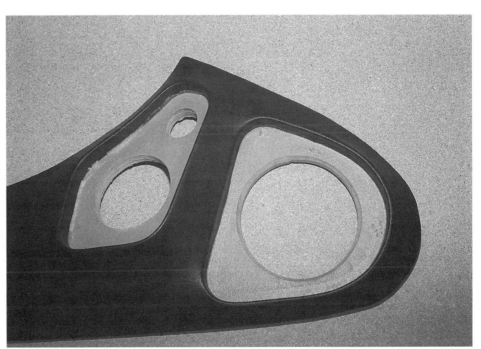

Close up shows how the vinyl is contoured perfectly to the panel without any wrinkles. Note how the covering wraps over the lip at each opening and is trimmed off just short of the bottom.

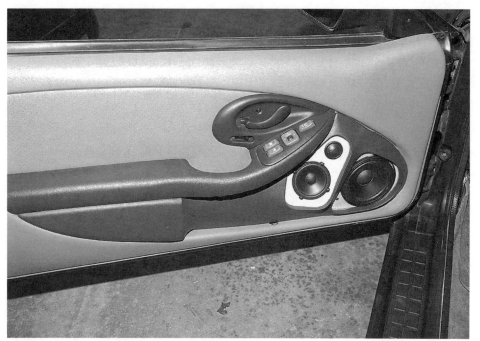

Here we see the installed panels before the grills are installed. Once the grills are installed people will want to know if the three speaker installation is a factory option.

This shot shows two of the three subwoofers and one of the external amplifiers. Note the all-range "rear fill" speaker used above the wheel well and the way it's been mounted to particle board.

computers, refrigerators, small appliances, stereos, TVs. Most of the time they've been in the audio field for a long time and have very good product knowledge. So unless you're going in to buy a certain piece you're much better off going to a small retail store.

Once I know how much money I have, then how do you advise me in terms of how I spend my money?

When you're budgeting out the money to do the stereo system, probably 50% of it is going to go to the electronics. The head unit and amplifiers, because that's the parts that take the most money to produce. The biggest thing to look for is the features that you want in a receiver because that's what you're going to be using. You don't play with the amps or the speakers - that's where the music comes out. You're going to be using the volume controls, bass and treble controls on the CD player or cassette deck itself.

Everybody has certain features that they're looking for. Most head units now have separate bass and treble controls, fader, front to rear, balance, the volume and all that are built into almost every radio. You have certain features, like a best station memory, so if you're not familiar with the area you're in you push a button and it automatically gets the six strongest stations. They all have presets so you can set your favorite stations.

Some head units have a subwoofer output so you don't have to have an external crossover for the subwoofers. Some of them are high-powered, front and rear, have one set of pre-outs to use for a single amp. There's a lot of things to consider, small features in the radios that some people are not familiar with.

And the other 50%?

You need 20-30% of the total for the speakers and the rest for your installation. For an ordinary system, that would be typical. Now if you're talking a custom installation where you

After the material is stapled in place Kelly brushes on epoxy resin with catalyst (no fiberglass mat is used at this time). Once the resin is set up the top of the enclosure will be a solid piece.

The top of the speaker enclosure consists of three large diameter rings cut from particle board. The first step in finishing the top is to to stretch speaker grille material across the entire piece.

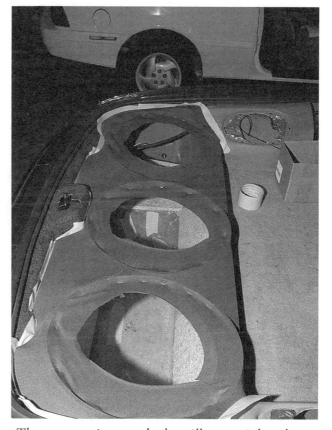

The next step is to staple the grille material to the wooden framework and cut excess material out of the center of each speaker hole. This is the same basic process used to create the door panels.

To strengthen the top of the enclosure Kelly cuts fiberglass mat into small rectangles, saturates each one with resin and catalyst and then sets it in place.

Here you can see how the small rectangles are pushed into place at the "openings" between the large rings and then coated with more resin.

want speakers hidden behind panels or custom enclosures, of course your installation labor is going to be higher.

When do you recommend a separate amp? What are the advantages of the separate amp?

With a separate amp you'll have a cleaner sound and it'll be able to play louder. An amplifier has a separate power supply. The radio doesn't. You use a pre-amp signal from the radio which produces the voltage. The amplifier will amplify the voltage and turn it into wattage. You can go anywhere from 20 watts to 500 or 600 watts. Of course, for your full range speakers you don't need that much power, but it's the same idea as an engine. The more power you have, the faster you're going to go. The more wattage you have the louder it's going to be.

Deciding how much power you need depends on the total system and your personal listening requirements?

It depends on your personal requirements *and* on the vehicle. Some vehicles, the street rods for example, they're going to be loud because they have big engines and you're going to have to overcome the sound of the motor to hear your system.

How do you match the speakers to the system?

The larger the speaker the lower the frequency it will handle of course, and the smaller the speaker the high-

sive speaker is going to sound better, but if you're comfortable with the sound of your speaker, that's what you're looking for. Instead of a salesman telling you, 'these are the best speakers we have, buy these,' - well, if you're not using a 150 watt amp, you don't need 150 watt speakers. The speaker does not produce wattage. It has a power handling rating. So if you're asking for a speaker that's a 150 watt speaker, you're asking for the power han-

Kelly goes through the process of adding fiberglass mat to the triangular shaped openings three or four times to create the necessary strength.

er the frequencies that it will handle. The crossover determines which frequency goes to which speakers. Some amplifiers have low or high-pass filters that do the job of the crossover.

You should remember that a particular speaker is going to sound different to you than it does to me. Some people have hearing loss in the higher frequencies, or hearing loss in certain areas, or they simply know what type of sound they want. You go into a store and you listen to the different types of speakers and you find what you're looking for. If you're using just a radio for power, you won't have any problem with a speaker that's made to handle up to 30 watts. If you're using an amplifier that's 50 watts per channel, you need a speaker that's going to handle that kind of power. But the important thing is, I cannot tell you which speaker sounds better to you. I can only tell you which one sounds better to me.

So I have to pick what sounds best?

Yeah. There are different price ranges in speakers. You'll find three different categories. But if you know how much wattage you're going to use, that'll tell you which category you should be in. For sound quality, of course, the more expen-

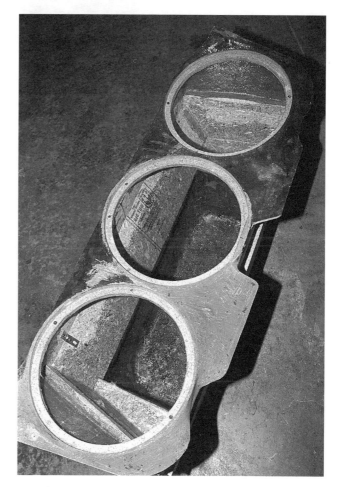

At this point the top section (placed on top of the enclosure box) is partly sanded prior to installation of trim adhesive and the vinyl.

dling of the speaker, not the output of the speaker.

Is it actually a detriment to use a 150 or 200 watt speaker in a system that's only got half that much power? I mean you're wasting money, but beyond that.

To a point it is, because the speaker has a sensitivity rating. It will produce a certain volume with a certain amount of power. If you're under-powering a speaker, it's not going to play as loud. You're trying to make it play loud-

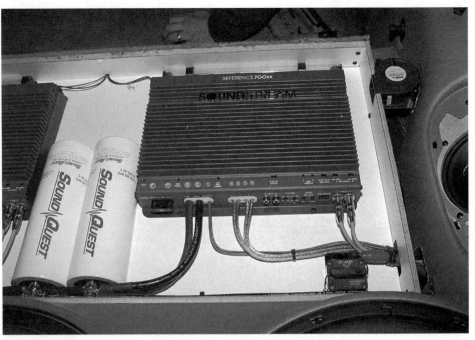

The REF 700 amp drives the door and rear-fill speakers. A small fan in the upper right will keep air moving through the box once it's covered. At the lower right is the fuse for the second battery.

Fully installed, the three subwoofers, two amplifiers and their enclosure, and the "rear" speakers with grille covers.

er with less power and you will encounter clipping more easily as a result. Clipping means you're squaring off the signal waves which will blow up the speaker. With clipping, a sine wave turns into a square wave.

What kinds of mistakes do people make when they buy stereos or put stereos in their car?

They don't think ahead. If they're thinking ahead, they'll buy the head unit that they're looking for. They might spend a couple more bucks to get the features, but six months down the road they're not going to kick themselves and say, 'Oh man, I should have bought that other one because I like these features better.' Sometimes they end up buying cheaper speakers to fit into a budget when six months down the road, they wish they bought the better speakers. Don't buy something and end up replacing it. Instead, try to wait and hold off. Maybe buy it a piece at a time but get the piece you really want.

It helps to come to somebody like you who can kind of walk you through the process, help with the planning part of the deal?

It does help if you find the right person. If

you find a salesperson that is just a salesperson, they might know the features, but they don't know the system. If you're looking at building a car, you have so many different areas - you have the engine, the transmission, the tires, etc. in the complete car. A stereo system is the same idea. You have so many different areas to consider, you have to match them to each other to get the desired final result. The salesman who's not familiar with the entire system is going to sell you features. They're not going to sell you an end result.

Is there anything you'd like to cover, in terms of the considerations a person has to make when he or she buys a complete system?

A lot of people are going to be talked into more than they need. They're going to go into a store and a salesperson is going to sell them on the more expensive speakers or the more expensive amplifiers. The customer has to go in knowing what they're looking for and not let the salesman push them into spending more money than necessary. If you know you're going to listen to the system this loud and you're not going to be turning it up over that volume you probably don't need an amplifier on your main speakers - so don't buy one. The built in amplifier on the CD players or cassette decks now is fairly clean. You don't have to have an external amp to your main speakers if you're not real concerned with the volume. But your four inch speakers are not going to play down to a lower bass frequency so if you're looking for something to play down to 50 Hertz, normally you need to add a subwoofer of some sort.

If I don't need a subwoofer how much do I have to spend for a good stereo system?

If you don't need a subwoofer, and you're looking at just the high powered radio and front and rear speakers, it will range from a low end of $500 or $600 installed, up to as much as you want to spend. You can always spend more because speakers start at $69 a pair and go to $400 a pair, so it's hard to say. Remember that you can always do a head unit, all four speakers without an amplifier

and later add an amp. That's another step.

You buy the speakers because you like the way they sound. Then you buy the head unit with the features you need. Six months down the road you have more money. Now you can either put in an amplifier to make the system louder, or you can buy an amp and a subwoofer which will produce the bass you're not getting,.

If we get into the subwoofers that's a line of demarcation in terms of price?

It's very easy to make a very clean sounding system with the subwoofer and a separate amp for $1,500 or $1,600.

Kelly Kitzman and his personal-project-Cadillac in the showroom at Sound Waves. After 10 years in the business Kelly likes the installations that people say "can't be done."

Chapter seven

Fuel Injection

Buy and install the right harness

More and more hot rods are turning up with fuel injection under the hood. Besides that certain sex appeal offered by a polished TPI unit, there are some definite benefits to fuel injection in terms of power, driveability and a clean tail pipe.

In order to help you understand these systems, decide which might be the best for your situation, and buy the right harness, this Fuel Injection chapter offers a short history (see the side-bar on page 88), a look at current fuel injec-

G.M. Tuned Port Injection units come in two versions, mass-air or speed-density. This monochromatic installation, with the air filter mounted right up front, is a speed-density unit.

tion systems offered by the factories, and a typical installation sequence. This chapter deals primarily with adaptation of factory fuel injection systems (mostly G.M.) to hot rod use and does not cover the stand alone high performance fuel injection systems available from the aftermarket.

For the street rodder or enthusiast who wants to run factory style fuel injection, this chapter should make it easier to buy the system, choose a good matching wiring harness, and install the harness.

Late model LT-1 type fuel injection with the factory covers help make for an extremely sanitary engine compartment. Rodder's Digest

TODAY'S HIGH PERFORMANCE FACTORY FUEL INJECTION

The current fuel injection systems used by both Ford and G.M. in their high performance V-8s are port type injection with electronic control. There is one fuel injector for each cylinder, mounted in the intake manifold just upstream from the intake valve. Some use a "ninth" injector to inject fuel during cold starts.

As with earlier systems, each injector is actually a solenoid. G.M. injectors fire once per crankshaft revolution. The electronic control module (ECM) determines the pulse width, or how long the injector will stay open. Fuel injection systems from G.M. can be broken down according to (cont'd on page 92)

G.M. crate motors can be ordered in various configurations, including engines with the complete fuel injection system already installed.

History of Fuel Injection

FUEL INJECTION — SOME EARLY HISTORY AND BACKGROUND

Most of the early fuel injection prototypes used by engineer and aircraft designers during and before WWII used direct injection with mechanical controls. Direct injection uses a very high pressure pump (over 1000 PSI) to inject fuel directly into the cylinder. Many of these designs were actually converted diesel injection systems.

One of the first post-war applications of fuel injection came in 1949 when the first fuel injected Offenhauser appeared at Indianapolis. The system was designed by Stuart Hilborn and Bill Travers, by 1953 this system was standard equipment on Offy powered cars.

The system came to be known as Hilborn fuel injection and soon crossed over into other types of racing. The Hilborn system differed from others - this was *indirect* (or port-type) injection, with fuel injected into the intake port just ahead of the intake valve. The port injection design meant fuel could be sprayed at a much lower pressure, eliminating the expensive and noisy high-pressure fuel pump.

At about the same time G.M. began researching practical applications of this new fuel injection technology. Zora Arkus Duntov teamed up with John Dolza, another G.M. engineer, to design a fuel injection system for the Corvette. Zora and John chose a port injection system with mostly mechanical controls. The key to any good fuel injection system is the precise measurement of the air mass entering the engine so the correct amount of fuel can be injected. The early system built by Rochester measures the air mass as it first enters the engine.

The new Rochester fuel injection system was introduced on the 1957 Corvette. Pontiac, in an attempt to keep up with the corporate Joneses, offered the same system on some Bonnevilles. Over 2,000 fuel injected Corvettes were sold during 1957. Unfortunately, the Rochester system worked better in the lab than it did in practice. Chevrolet offered the Rochester system until 1965 but only in very limited numbers.

Installed here in a 1957 Chevy Nomad, the early Rochester fuel injection systems used mechanical controls of the port-type system.

History of Fuel Injection

About the time G.M. was eliminating fuel injection from the options list, a few European manufacturers were looking into the use of fuel injection as standard equipment.

THE EVOLUTION OF MODERN FUEL INJECTION SYSTEMS

During the mid-1960's, Volkswagen asked the Robert Bosch company to design a fuel injection system capable of meeting future U.S. emissions standards.

This new system was a port or indirect fuel injection system. What made the system unique was the complete electronic control. Fuel was injected by solenoid type injectors mounted just upstream of the intake valves. The length of each injection pulse was determined by an early Electronic Control Module (the computer).

Rather than try to sample the amount of the air mass directly, Bosch used RPM and vacuum sensors (to determine engine speed and load) to give an approximation of total mass air. The control module used this indirect mass air measurement, modified by inputs from temperature and throttle position sensors, to determine the timing and duration of each injection pulse. More sophisticated examples of this same basic system are still used on many vehicles today. Systems that rely on this indirect means of measuring total air are known as *speed-density* systems.

FUEL INJECTION THEORY

The goal of any fuel delivery system is to deliver the right proportion of fuel and air to the cylinder in a combustible condition. Books tell us a ratio of 14.7 parts air to 1 part gasoline is an ideal, or "stoichiometric" ratio. The fuel delivery engineer is faced with a series of problems. First, the ideal ratio isn't always the same. Cold engines need a richer mixture, accelerating engines need a little extra fuel to maximize power. Second, for complete combustion the gasoline must atomize and mix thoroughly with the air. Third, the correct ratio must be delivered under a variety of conditions, including temperature extremes and cornering forces.

Another port system with mechanical controls, the Hilborn fuel injection system enjoyed great popularity on a variety of competition cars during the 1950s and 1960s. Rodder's Digest

History of Fuel Injection

Before examining fuel injection, it might help to look at the alternative - carburetors. At the heart of most carburetors is a venturi. A venturi is simply a restriction in a pipe, physics demands that as the air speeds up to pass through the venturi, the pressure drops. Gasoline, under atmospheric pressure in the float bowl, is pushed through the jet and into the opening in the venturi, where it mixes with the air.

Presuming we have the correctly mixed ratio of air and gas, the mixture must still travel through the intake manifold to each cylinder. The path from carburetor to cylinder is seldom straight. The relative weight of gasoline becomes a problem as the mixture makes those tight turns, and the gas sometimes separates from the air stream and puddles in the manifold runners.

The net result of all this is a system that fails on occasion to provide an ideal air fuel mixture and has further trouble delivering that ideal mixture to each cylinder.

Fuel injection offers a number of advantages when compared to carburetion; some of these advantages are inherent in the design, others are the result of modern day computer technology.

At the heart of the system are the injectors themselves. Gasoline must be mixed with air before it will burn. The mist created by the injection nozzles breaks the gasoline into very, very small particles. Smaller particles mix more readily with the air. Equally important, a very small particle is more likely to obtain enough oxygen for complete combustion. Complete combustion means more power and fewer waste products at the tailpipe.

Because this fuel mist is delivered just upstream from the intake valve, there is no problem of separation of fuel and air in the intake manifold. The throttle body can be sized for maximum performance, not for good air velocity in the intake tract.

Modern port injection systems tie all the injectors into a common fuel ring. Using a solenoid for an injector and controlling the solenoid with an electronic control module means great precision in delivering just

Modern fuel injectors, whether from Bosch or Rochester, are essentially solenoids, able to open and close in mili-seconds. Though modern injectors may look alike they may flow different capacities and should be matched to the individual engine.

History of Fuel Injection

exactly the correct amount of fuel. Modern systems do a very good job of measuring the air mass. That mass air measurement, coupled with information from temperature, RPM and throttle position sensors enables the control module to deliver a mixture exactly correct for a given set of engine conditions.

The precision is further fine tuned through the use of an oxygen sensor. The sensor samples the oxygen content in the exhaust and signals the control module if the mixture becomes too rich or too lean.

Most readers are interested in fuel injection as an aftermarket addition to their hot rod. But before trying to determine which system is best for your application, it might help to look over the new systems in some detail.

Because most of the engines - and thus most of the fuel injection systems - being bolted into street rods and hot rods are from G.M., it seems best to stay with a description of that system. Unless otherwise noted, the following comments on factory systems refer to the various G.M. EFI systems.

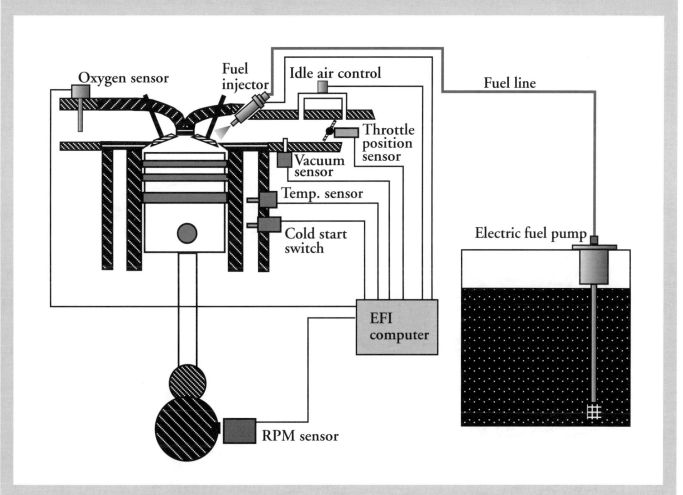

This simplified diagram shows the essentials of most electronic, port-type fuel injection systems. Shown is a speed-density system. RPM, vacuum, throttle position, temperature and exhaust sensors provide information to the computer which then decides when and for how long the injector should be open.

how they measure the air mass entering the engine. Some of the earlier systems, from 1985 to 1989, used a direct measure of the air mass and are known as *mass air* systems. Starting in 1990, G.M. switched to a *speed-density* system that relies on indirect measurement of the air mass entering the engine.

The latest systems from G.M. are actually a hybrid, a combined mass-air/speed-density system that uses both a MAF (mass air flow) and a MAP (manifold absolute pressure) sensor.

People often ask, which is the best system? There is no best, like anything else each system has advantages and disadvantages, especially when viewed from the unique perspective of a hot rodder.

The speed-density system uses a sophisticated electronic vacuum gauge known as a manifold absolute pressure sensor (or MAP) to measure the load on the engine. This MAP sensor, in combination with rpm information and inputs from temperature and throttle position sensors, provides the basic information the ECM needs to determine pulse width and timing.

With a mass-air system, the amount of air entering the engine is measured directly. The mass air flow sensor (MAF), sometimes known as a hot wire, measures the resistance of a piece of platinum wire in the intake tract. The wire is heated by current from the ECM, air moving past the wire tends to cool it, changing the resistance of the wire. This change in resistance is interpreted by the ECM as a change in air flow. In addition to the signal from the mass air sensor, these systems use inputs from throttle position, air temperature and RPM before determining the amount and timing of the injection pulse.

The ECM in either type of system is able

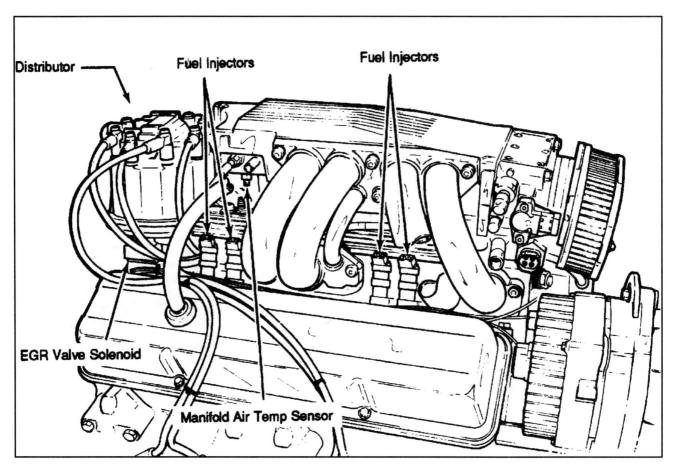

TPI units like this use a conventional distributor, individual runners and one injector per cylinder. Painless Wiring

to fine tune the amount of fuel being injected by analyzing its own exhaust sample. The oxygen sensor mounted in the exhaust system provides a signal to the ECM signaling any need for more or less fuel. This feedback or self-regulating mode used during idle and cruise situations is known as "closed loop." Open loop then describes those conditions, like wide open throttle, when the ECM operates without the input of the oxygen sensor.

EFI has a few more tricks up its fuel-injected sleeve: like control of idle speed through an idle air control and control of the ignition timing. Because the ECM knows engine speed and load (as well as air and engine temperature, and throttle position), it is in a very good position to determine the appropriate ignition timing. Through the use of a knock sensor the ECM is able to pick an ideal ignition timing figure and then roll it back slightly if that optimum figure results in a knock (another self-regulating feature).

The major difference in the two types of EFI systems - in a real world sense - is that the speed-density EFI is designed and programmed to work with a very specific engine. These systems only know how much fuel to add during a given situation because they've been "mapped." The map provided by the factory dictates that a given set of conditions creates a particular pulse width. If you change the camshaft or add a set of headers the amount of air moving through that engine changes, but the map remains the same. Yes, you can change the map (contained on the PROM - more about PROMs later) but it can be tough to get just the right map for your particular set of modifications.

A mass-air type of system might be better suited to people who want to modify their

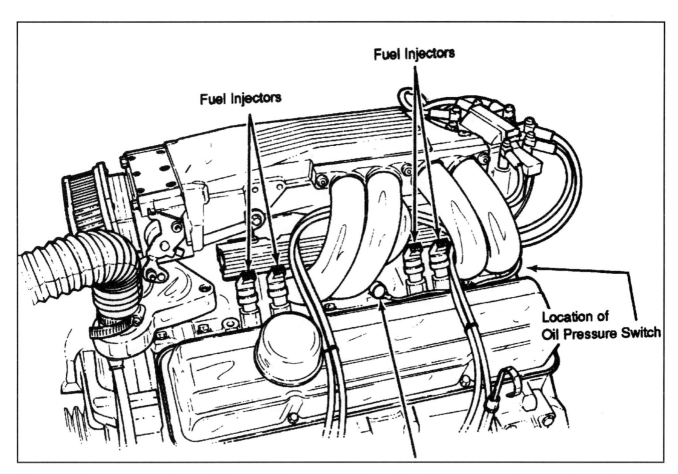

The left side of this speed density TPI engine shows the location of the oil pressure switch - not to be confused with an oil pressure sender. Painless Wiring

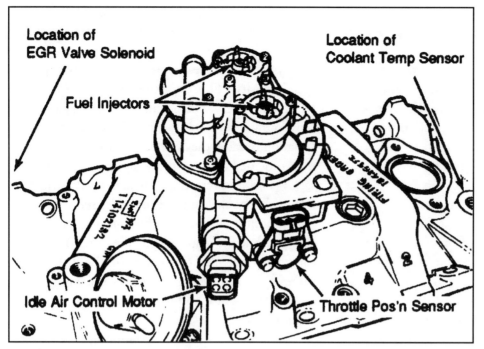

Throttle body fuel injection, as used in many truck applications, is really nothing more than two electronic fuel injectors mounted in a throttle body that takes the place of the carburetor. Painless Wiring

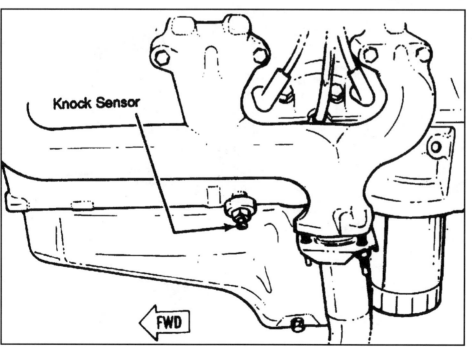

Mounted on the engine's left side, the knock sensor is an essential part of any EFI installation. When buying parts for your fuel injected engine, it's important to use the correct part numbers so all the components are compatible.

engines, because any increase in airflow, caused by a new camshaft for example, will automatically create additional fuel (note: in this scenario you may still have to get a new aftermarket chip that will provide optimum timing for the new modified engine).

At this point it might be instructive to describe the ECM, computer, or black box that drives these modern fuel injection systems.

The computer truly is a black box, black in the sense that it is sealed from any tinkering on our part. The only part you can readily change is the PROM (programmable read only memory). The PROM contains the specific timing and fuel injection instructions for each specific model of car. By installing an aftermarket PROM (sometimes known as a chip) you are able to change the amount and timing of the injection pulse under certain conditions as well as the ignition timing and curve. The PROM also contains the VATS information (Vehicle Anti-Theft), meaning that unless you use the key and lock cylinder that came out of the new car you will again need an aftermarket PROM.

Also contained in the computer is the Cal Pak or calibration package. The Cal Pak contains the instruction for the "limp-home" mode. Limp home is one of the computer's three basic operating modes (the other two being open-loop and closed-loop). Limp-home is the mode the computer operates in when it senses a major malfunction. In this mode, the computer uses a very limited fuel curve and limits ignition timing to a total of twenty-two degrees.

WHAT'S OUT THERE - Current G.M. systems and how to tell them apart

The three most common EFI systems currently being used on hot rods are:

1. Throttle body fuel injection, used on cars and trucks from about 1987 to the present.

2. The Tuned Port fuel injection system (TPI) used on both 305 and 350 cubic inch engines. This system came in early and late versions. The early version, from 1985 to 1989, used a computer with two electrical plug ins, a ninth injector for cold starts and a MAF (mass air flow) sensor to directly measure the volume of incoming air.

The later 1990 to 1992 TPI systems use a computer with three electrical plug ins, no ninth injector, and a MAP (Manifold Absolute Pressure) sensor instead of a MAF sensor. These are speed-density systems.

3. The LT-1 system, used from 1992 through 1993, which looks totally different than a TPI system, uses its own computer, no conventional distributor and an oxygen sensor in both sides of the exhaust. The LT-1 uses a MAP sensor and is a speed-density system.

4. The newest system from G.M., the LT-1/LT-4 used from 1994 to 1996 is a combined mass-air/speed-density system with both MAF and MAP sensors. There are few aftermarket wiring systems on the market so we do not discuss this system.

Various computers have been used over the years on G.M. systems. On the right is a 7730, used with speed-density systems from '90 to '92. On the left, a 7165, used with mass-air TPI systems from '86 to '89 (numbers refer to the last 4 digits of the part number).

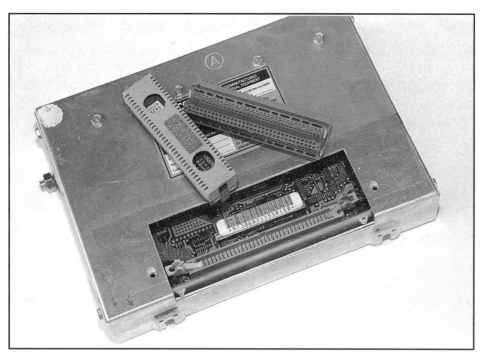

The prom, or "chip" plugs in to the computer and carries much of the information needed for correct operation.

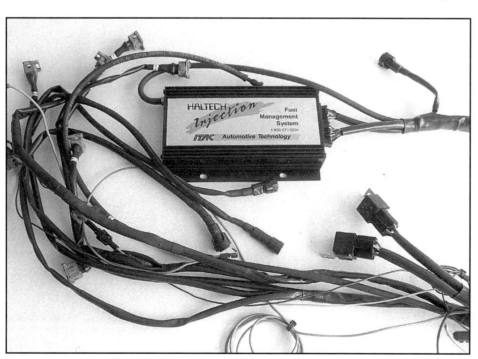

Stand-alone systems like this from Haltech use their own computer and their own wiring harness.

"The easiest way to distinguish the system you have," explains Brian Montgomery, from Painless Wiring, "is by checking the computer that came with the engine. The early one has two plugs (early tuned port (1986-89) and the later TPI system has three plugs (1990 -1992)."

BEFORE YOU BRING ONE HOME

EFI motors are common at the junk yard or the swap meets these days. Bringing one home is easy, and a variety of wiring and installation kits make the conversion to hot rod use very straightforward. In spite of all these aids there are a few mistakes people make on a regular basis. Mistakes that make the job of installing a fuel injected engine in your car or truck much tougher and more expensive than it needs to be.

Brian Montgomery explains that the first thing people need to do when they buy an engine is to be sure the motor they buy is really complete. "The buyer needs to get as many parts as possible when they buy the engine, to make sure it really is complete. That way you save the time and trouble of chasing parts, and the expense of buying them. Most important, you know that the parts on the engine are the right ones. People get a motor that's missing some parts and they try to mix and match relays and sensors and it really screws everything up. When they call here we explain that they must follow the parts list that comes with our instructions to the letter. But the easiest way is to just buy an engine that comes with the computer, the distributor (for non-LT-1 engines) and all the right sensors and relays."

Another common topic on the Painless Tech Line is the relative advantage of the mass-air or speed-density systems. To quote Brian again, "I think the mass-air system, as used on the early TPI units, is better because you can make more modifications to the engine and the system will automatically compensate. With mass-air it's measuring the amount of air. With speed-density, if you make very many changes you need to have a custom chip burned from a company like Hypertech and some others. A speed-density system can self regulate to some extent but it's limited. I tell people with a speed-density engine that it's better to leave the engine stock."

"You need to know how you want to run the engine (mass-air or speed-density) before you buy an engine. That way you will get the correct equipment right away, including the right computer. It can be tough to convert from one system to the other, it's easier to just get what you want right away."

"There are a few quirks too. Like the 1985 TPI engine. These are all by

Not all HEI distributors are created equal. On the left with screw-down mounting lugs is a distributor meant for a TPI engine with all the right plug ins.

Mounted here behind a Corvette ZR-1 motor, the 700/R4 transmission uses the engine computer to control torque converter lock up.

themselves, the computer and everything else is different. But the engine is the same, so you can use the 1986 and later harness, computer and fuel injection parts on a 1985 engine."

COMMENTS FROM THE FIELD
A conversation with Doug Rippie

For some additional fuel injected advice we called on Doug Rippie from Doug Rippie Motorsport. Doug does a tremendous amount of fuel injection work on G.M. products, and sells a variety of upgrade components to increase the output of the various factory EFI systems.

Doug suggested that even though the early mass-air style TPI units will automatically correct fuel flow to compensate for changes in the cam or a pair of headers, you may still need to find and install a new computer chip. You may need a new chip that will provide the engine with a more appropriate curve for the ignition timing.

He also feels that modified motors sometimes benefit from a tuner or company that specializes in fuel injection work. A wide variety of chips are available, and companies like Doug's can often burn a custom chip for unique applications. In the case of the latest, 1994 and later, 700/R4 transmissions, the well equipped shop can go in through the computer and tune the transmission to the car, including correction to the speedometer and adjustment of each shift point.

Doug's final comments apply to all fuel injection installations, and mimic the advice already offered: "It's important to be sure you have good grounds for the computer and the rest of the system. If possible, get the power for the computer direct from the battery. Use welding cable instead of regular battery cable, it has many more strands and will carry the current with little or no voltage drop. This is very important with a fuel injected car, especially when the battery is mounted in the back of the car or in the trunk."

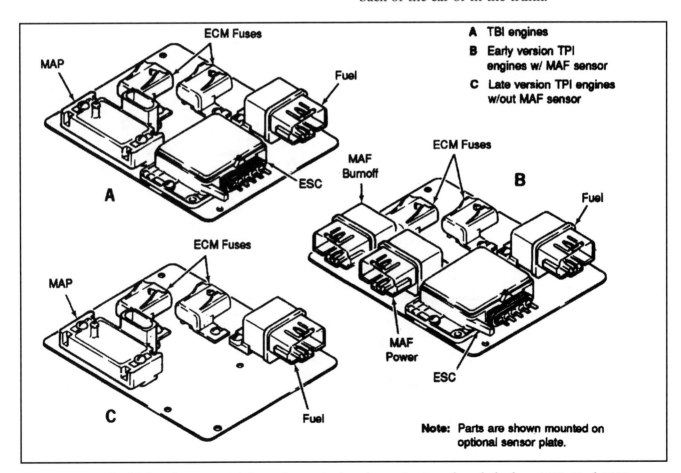

How many, and which, relays are used depends on whether the engine is a throttle body or TPI. Each TPI system is different as well. Painless Wiring

Hands-On:
A step-by-step conversion from carburetor to Tuned Port Injection

The following article documents the conversion of a Chevy pickup truck from carburetion to fuel injection. Though the story has an off-road flavor, installation would be the same if the vehicle were an early Camaro or an even earlier small-block equipped street rod. We are grateful to Gary Medley for both the story and the photos.

CHEVY TUNED PORT CONVERSION: PERFORMANCE AT ANY ANGLE

For your average, dirt-under-the-fingernails 4x4 owner, the ultimate off-road experience is maneuvering up and down the steepest slope possible. And if he could pull it off, driving upside down through a back-country tunnel would be even better.

Unfortunately, such a feat is out of the questions for most 4x4s. You see, carburetors only operate at a certain angle before the float mechanism moves out if its range of motion — and stops delivering fuel. Not a pleasant experience when inching up a steep incline — or in that tunnel.

Ah, but there's a better way: Convert your carb-fed small-block to fuel injection. Fuel injection, whether it's throttle body (like on a zillion stock pickups) or tuned-port injection (Camaros and Corvettes), operates at any vehicle angle — even upside down. Gravity isn't a factor. (Well, maybe for the oil pump...)

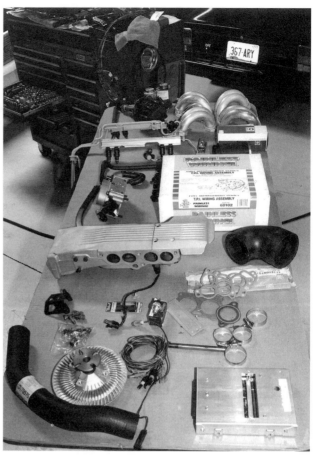

Before beginning the job, Arizona TPI organized all the parts on one table — simplifies the process and saves time.

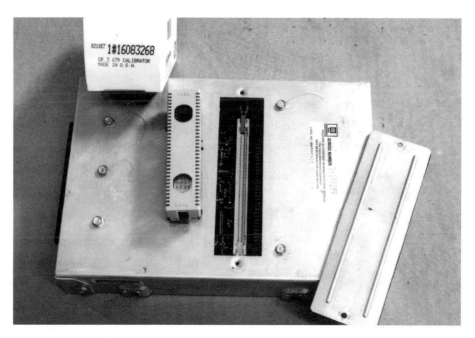

The brains of this outfit — the ECM out of a 1986-88 Camaro (p/n 01227165, later upgraded to p/n 16198259). Arizona TPI also recommends the 1988 350 TPI "PROM" chip (AC Delco p/n 16083268)

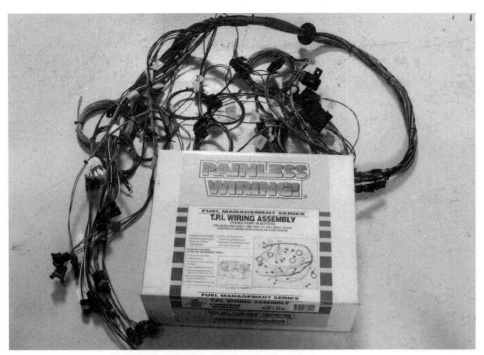

The Painless Wiring TPI fuel injection harness includes everything you need to connect your system. The comprehensive instruction manual includes a complete list of all parts required, with GM part numbers.

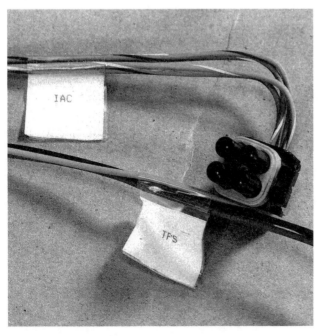

Painless Wiring identifies every wiring circuit and connector with small plastic flags. Do NOT remove these tags until you are finished!

So, if you're a serious off-roader with a carb-fed 350 — Chevy 4x4 pickup, Jeep, Land Cruiser, whatever — and make a habit of scaling sheer rock faces, fuel injection is for you. To see how fuel injection can work for off-roaders, we contacted the folks at Arizona TPI in Tempe, Ariz. Owner Ed Newton and his team are experts at GM fuel injection systems. (Ed used to manage automotive products for Intel. He knows his way around a circuit board.) Recently, Arizona TPI converted a carb-equipped 1971 Chevy 4x4 pickup to a GM tuned-port fuel injection system. We followed along to show that such a conversion can be handled by the average wrench-savvy 4x4 owner.

GM tuned-port fuel was introduced in 1985 on the 5.0-liter Camaro and the 5.7 liter Corvette powerplants. These systems employed a Bosch MAF (mass air flow) sensor to monitor the amount of air entering the engine. In 1991-1992, both 5.0- and 5.7-liter tuned-port systems relied upon a MAP (manifold absolute pressure) sensor to determine the volume of air entering the motor. These are known as "speed-density" systems. 1992 also saw Chevrolet introduce the LT1 small-block with a new version of TPI, producing increased power and torque. These days, most carb-EFI conversions use the standard TPI systems, either MAF or speed density. On our 1971 Chevy 4x4, Arizona TPI installed a MAF tuned-port system.

A TPI fuel injection system requires the following components: TPI intake manifold and air plenum, throttle body, computer (a.k.a., ECM for electronic control module), GM electronically controlled distributor, electric fuel pump, fuel filter and pressure-safe post-pump filter, fuel return line to tank, MAF sensor, Electric Spark Control Module, fuel pump relay, coolant temperature sensor, knock sensor, oxygen sensor, oil pressure switch, vehicle speed sensor, and a wiring harness from Painless Wiring.

There are four basic steps in the conversion: swap the intake manifolds and distributors, re-mount accessories, mount the fuel pump and fuel lines, and route and connect the wiring harness and computer.

Switching manifolds and distributors was straightforward, although care must be taken when assembling the air plenum so that no air leaks occur. Also, GM uses "Torx" fasteners, requiring an extra trip to the tool store. Next up, fuel pump, filters, and fuel lines were mounted. On our truck, we decided to make life easy by mounting the fuel pump and filters outside the stock tank. (On late-model GM cars the pump is inside the tank.) TPI systems run at a high pressure, between 45-50 psi. Arizona TPI uses as much hard-fuel line as possible, but connections can be made with high-pressure fuel injection hose and worm clamps. The pump itself is a roller-vane type pump that spins at 3,500 RPM.

The next step was running the return line into the tank. The return tube should be within one inch of the tank bottom, ensuring that the tube opening is always submersed under the fuel level. Ed and company added an extra tube through the stock fuel-tank sending unit mounting plate for the return line.

With the fuel pump, filters, and lines in place, we tackled the wiring. We spread out the Painless Wiring harness to make sense of the wires and oddball connectors that sprouted everywhere. Like all Painless Wiring harnesses, all connectors and sections are identified by small tags. Do not remove any tags until you are completely finished. Study the harness. Read the directions. Twice. Three times. Get a sense of how it all works before you connect or snip any wires!

The harness routing is contingent on where the computer is placed. We mounted ours to the bottom of the glovebox. Behind a kick panel or on the firewall are other logical spots. If you're totally out of space, Painless Wiring makes an extra long harness for placing the computer under the seat.

Next, we drilled a 1-5/8-inch hole in the firewall to slip the harness into the engine com-

Step one in converting from carb to TPI is installing the new intake manifold. Use a torque wrench and the proper tightening sequence for a leak-free installation.

Before drilling the firewall hole for wiring harness, we roughly routed the harness, running the sensor connectors across the top of the manifold. Only then did we know where to best drill the hole.

Painless pre-assembles a rubber grommet for the harness to pass through. Note use of nylon zip ties every 3-4 inches to organize the harness.

Before fuel rail and air runner and plenum are installed, we carefully routed sensor wires atop the manifold. This makes for a neat installation, as wires are hidden under the plenum.

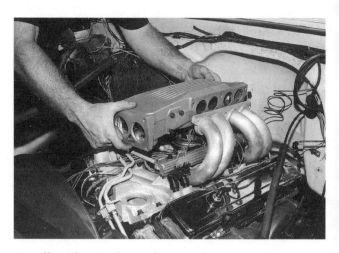

Installing the air plenum between the runners.

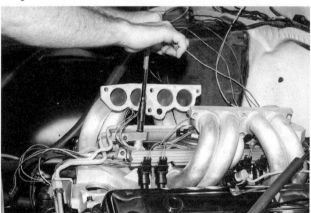

We set the fuel rails and runners in place before tightening the rails. Be sure not to pinch injector wires.

The throttle body does more than let air into the plenum. Note the three hoses: top is breather/fresh-air vent; middle is vacuum source; bottom is for coolant. Do not over tighten the throttle body bolts, as it can warp the casting and/or squeeze out the gasket.

If you use the correct Torx head factory fasteners to attach the air runners, you'll need to purchase an extra long 3/8" drive T-40 tool. Mac Tools p/n SC161. At this point, do not completely tighten the runners, since the plenum must slide between them.

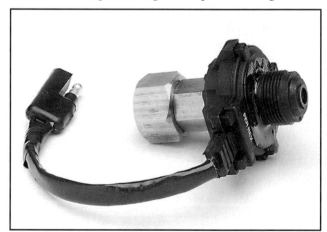

Vehicle speed sensor from Painless Wiring attaches between the transmission and speedometer cable. It tells the computer (ECM) the relative speed of the car.

partment. This is easily the most bewildering moment. There are seemingly a zillion connectors — all different. We carefully fished them through the hole and arranged them in their general positions. All connectors are unique to the sensor they feed. You can't hook them up wrong. Making it all look neat, though, is a time consuming process. Take your time.

A couple of these sensors require special attention. The vehicle speed sensor is a little gismo that tells the computer the relative speed your car is traveling. It screws into the speedometer cable outlet on the transmission. The oxygen sensor monitors exhaust gas content. It goes into the exhaust system within 12 inches of an exhaust port. We drove our Chevy (carburetor and all) to a local muffler shop, which welded the threaded boss into the downpipe just below the exhaust manifold mounting flange. By doing this first, we avoided unbolting any part of the exhaust system.

With all engine compartment sensors and wires hooked up, we turned our attention under the dash. We found homes for the fuel-pump relay, fuses, ESC (electronic spark control) and ALDL connector. The ALDL — what? ALDL stands for Assembly Line Diagnostic Link, a small 12-pin connector used to retrieve diagnostic error codes that are stored in the computer. Painless Wiring mounts the ALDL on a small bracket with a small "check engine" light. This light comes on when

Oxygen sensor screws into a boss welded into the exhaust system, within 12 inches of an exhaust port. Do this while the car is still running — so you can drive it to the muffler shop!

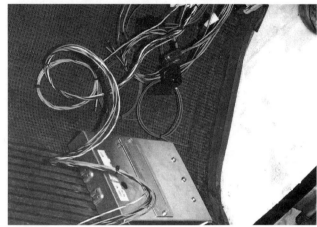

At this point, under the dash looks like the refuge bin at a pasta house. But don't be alarmed. When everything is complete, wires are tucked neatly away.

Arizona TPI modified the existing fuel tank pickup/gauge sending unit assembly for the fuel return line. The original feed line became the return line and a new pickup/feed line was fabricated and run through the new hole.

Fuel filter/pump assembly is attached inside frame rail directly under the fuel tank. On the right is the pre-filter, then the pump, then the fuel filter.

We mounted the ECM computer under the glove box. Kick panel or firewall are also good locations.

The completed TPI-equipped 350 Chevy.

the ignition is turned on and goes out once the engine fires — unless there is a problem. Then it stays illuminated, announcing there is a problem. If the problem is momentary, the light will go out, but the ECM will remember the error. To find out what happened, you jump two terminals on the ALDL, which causes the check-engine light to flash error codes. Yes, TPI talks to you. Then you simply fix the problem. Try that with a carburetor.

Finally, everything was connected, plumbed and mounted. We then primed the pump by loosening the fuel line until gas flowed out. We re-tightened the clamp. Next, we turned the key one click. The check engine light came on and the fuel pump cycled for two seconds. We engaged the starter, and the engine spun around about six seconds or so, fired right up and idled.

On the road, the Chevy exhibited crisp, flawless throttle response — no hesitations off the line, no cold-start stumble. In fact, to start the engine on a cold morning requires simply turning the key. The engine fires immediately and idles smoothly. On the road, fuel economy is up and driveability is improved. And re-jetting for changes in altitude is a thing of the past; the computer automatically adjusts fuel mixture.

There you have it — a quick primer on fuel injection. To describe fully all the nuances and technical background of fuel injection would take a book. And, in fact, there are several tomes that do just that: "Chevrolet TPI Swappers Guide" by John Baechtel, "How to Tune & Modify Chevrolet Fuel Injection" by Ben Watson, "Tuned Port Fuel Injection" by Choco Munday, and "Chevrolet TBI & TPI Engine Swapping" by Mike Knell. All are available from Motorbooks International (1-800-826-6600). All have comprehensive overviews of GM fuel injection basics plus extensive troubleshooting techniques.

Sources:
Arizona TPI
717 E. Hacienda Drive, #S105
Tempe, AZ 85281
602-921-2500

BEFORE YOU START
Installation tips

Most of the information that follows is taken from the Painless Wiring instruction manuals. We've included it here because, while some is specific to a Painless Wiring kit, much of this information is pertinent to the installation of nearly any G.M. fuel injection harness.

Prior to beginning the actual installation of the harness there are a few things to consider:
A. Are you going to use a 700/R4 Lockup Transmission and do you want the computer to control the lockup?
B. Does the engine have to be emissions legal i.e., does the EGR valve and/or air solenoid, and diverter valve need to be connected?

If you answered yes to *either or both* of these questions then you must connect the wires labeled VSS to a vehicle speed sensor that will pro-vide a four (4) pulse signal to the computer. On the Throttle Body and early model Tuned Port the sensor should output a square wave and on the late model Tuned Port engines it should provide a sine wave output. Painless Wiring offers the correct speed sensors for use with cable drive (mechanical) speedometers.

If you answered no to both of these questions then you do not have to use a vehicle speed sensor. Doug Rippie, however, suggests that everyone use a VSS because that's the only way the computer knows to switch to idle mode. Without the signal that the car has stopped moving the idle mixture is too rich.

If you are going to use a vehicle speed sensor then you will take the orange/black and black/white wires in the dash section (labeled for the park neutral indicator switch) and connect them to the Park/Neutral Indicator switch as

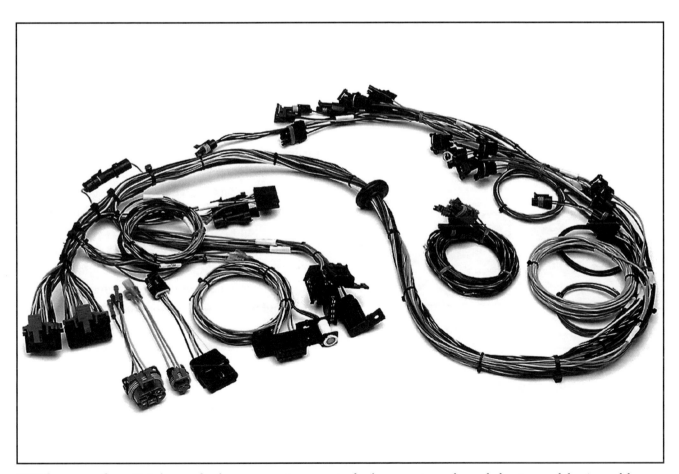

TPI harnesses from Painless and other companies come in both mass-air and speed-density models. A good harness uses high quality wire and connectors and has easy to read labels. Painless Wiring

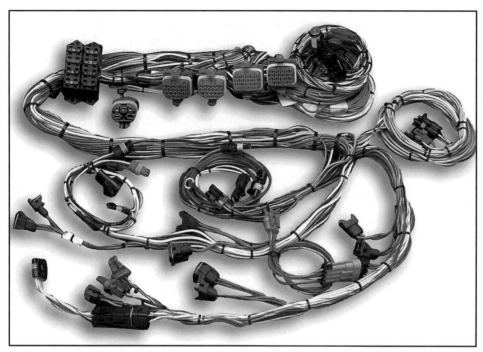

The LT-1 harness from Painless is meant for '92 and '93 engines. It can also be used on later LT-1 motors if the earlier, '92-'93, ECM is used. (Electronically controlled transmissions can not be used.)

Painless Wiring makes these adapters so an Oxygen sensor can be added to any exhaust system.

instructed. Do not connect the wires together.

Important: The instructions below supersede the instructions in the manual concerning the orange/black and black/white wires in the dash section that are labeled: For the park/neutral indicator switch. Under no circumstances should you connect these wires to a neutral safety switch. You should never connect the orange/black and black/white wires to the vehicle speed sensor wiring.

If you are not going to use a vehicle speed sensor then you will take the orange/black and black/white wires in the dash section (labeled for the park/neutral indicator switch) and connect the orange/black and black/white wires together.

If you do *not* wish to use the lockup function, tape off and store the single purple wire in the dash group and the 4-position square connector in the tail section.

If you are going to use the lockup circuit then you must have a vehicle speed sensor (VSS), and the correct brake switch. These are necessary to make the lockup function work correctly. The brake switch should be closed (electrically connected) when the brakes *are not* being applied and open (not electrically connected) when the brakes *are* being applied. This is the opposite of a standard brake light switch. The vehicle speed sensor lets the computer know how fast, and if, the wheels are turning.

Regardless of whether you use the lockup function, the vehicle speed sensor (VSS) is needed by the computer so that it can command the emissions control devices on the engine. This part is necessary if you want your vehicle to be street-legal. There are two different VSS harness applications.

LT-1 applications require use of either the factory VSS or the 60116 VSS from Painless.

All TBI and early TPI harnesses require three wires, a hot (B+) which may be spliced into the throttle position sensor gray wire (if no gray wire is in the VSS group) a ground, which may be spliced into any Blk/Wht wire or attached directly to ground, and a brown to computer signal. The late TPI has two wires, purple and yellow, that go to the sensor from the computer, no power wires are needed.

You should get to know the particular engine that you are using. G.M. throttle body injection (TBI) system: The engine and the 60101 and 60201 harness are designed to use a manifold absolute pressure (MAP) sensor and an electronic spark control (ESC) module as well as the other wiring that the computer needs to operate.

Early version tuned port injection (TPI) system with a mass-airflow (MAF) sensor: The 60102 and 60202 harness will support the mass airflow (MAF) sensor, the burn off circuit wiring, and the electronic spark control (ESC) module in addition to the other wiring common to the Tuned Port systems.

Late version tuned port injection (TPI) system without a mass airflow (MAF) sensor, designed to use a manifold absolute pressure (MAP) sensor, but does not require an electronic spark control (ESC) module: The 60103 and 60203 harnesses are designed for and will support this system. This system has three connectors at the computer.

With regard to computer chips, on late model (1990 and up) Tuned Port engines all factory chips have the vehicle anti-theft system (VATS)

You don't have to run a small-block Chevy motor if you want EFI. A variety of aftermarket kits are available to help you convert a Ford from carburetion to fuel injection.

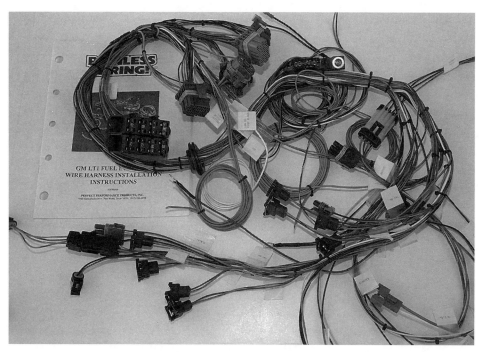

EFI harnesses are designed for a particular application. Be sure to match the harness, engine and type of EFI. Look for a harness with good components, thorough instructions and the services of a 800 number.

programmed into them so that they cannot be used unless the factory steering column, compatible with the computer, is installed. For the late model tuned port only, you must obtain an aftermarket chip that does not have the VATS programming in it. The chip part numbers listed in the compatible parts chart are the chips that we offer for your convenience, but you do not have to use a Painless Wiring chip.

For the late model tuned port systems, if you order a chip from someone other than Painless Wiring, you will need to obtain a chip that will be compatible with our harness and has the VATS removed.

Quality aftermarket harnesses like this from Painless include the check engine light.

INSTALLATION
DOs and DON'Ts

Caution: Do not disconnect the battery or the computer connector(s) while the ignition is on.

Do not short any wire in this harness to ground (with the exception of labeled ground wires) or damage to the computer will result. Giving or receiving a jump start may damage the computer.

Do not use a test light when testing computer sensors or circuits. Damage to the computer will result!

When routing the wires for the vehicle speed sensor (if used) make certain that they are at least 12 inches away from any ignition wiring (spark plug wires, etc.).

Note: All of the adapters listed in our manual are now included in the wiring kit. You should use or remove them depending on your particular application.

If you are switching a TPI motor from MAF Sensor to MAP Sensor then you must use the new knock sensor in the parts table.

An oil pressure *switch* (not a sender) must be used with this harness. Do not bypass oil pressure switch wires.

If you are using an oil pressure switch that has two or three small pins surrounded by a plastic collar for an electrical connection, an adapter is available from PPPI, part number 60107.

There is a normal, small current drain on these fuel injected systems.

Throttle body systems will *not* work with anything other than a *stock* camshaft.

On throttle body systems, the power steering override switch (if so equipped) must be wired in-line on the A/C compressor power wire.

If you have a throttle body system and your throttle position sensor is different from that shown on page 94, you can obtain an adapter (part number 60106) from PPPI.

Each connector in this harness is different and will not fit in the wrong place. Never force any connector.

When connecting the plugs to the computer *use extreme care* to make sure none of the pins in the computer are or become bent.

If you have a G.M. separate coil ignition system on your engine: an adapter is included in the kit from PPPI, (part number 60108).

For your distributor: you must provide a power wire (14 ga. minimum) that is HOT (+12V) when the ignition switch is in the *start and run* positions. Connect it to the terminal on the distributor cap labeled Bat or to the pink wire on the separate coil ignition system. This wire pro-

Be sure the harness you buy comes with easy to read labels and high quality OEM-style plugs.

vides power to the ignition coil. Your automobile will not start or run without it.

The timing connector for the ignition is near where the wiring harness splits off to go to the sensor board.

Check the fuel pump relay connector on the harness to see if it requires a style 1 or a style 2 relay. A style 2 adapter is included in the kit.

The fuel pump you are using MUST be rated at a minimum of 45 pounds PSI (per square inch) for tuned port systems or 15 pounds PSI for throttle body systems.

If you have headers you may have to relocate the knock sensor for proper clearance.

The oil pressure switch wires are designed to be connected to an oil pressure switch, not the oil pressure sending unit. An oil pressure sending unit is for a gauge or an indicator light and will only have one terminal on the top. The stock oil pressure switch is cigar shaped and has three terminals. If you wish to use the stock oil pressure switch then you will use the oil pressure switch adapter included with this kit. On the oil pressure switch adapter there are two wires that match the wire colors coming from our harness and there is also an extra wire. The extra wire is for the factory oil pressure gauge or indicator light, depending on what the switch was originally designed for. You may also obtain a smaller oil pressure switch if you have clearance problems with the original oil pressure switch. This type of switch has two male connectors that will plug directly into the harness.

Grounding the vehicle

A perfectly and beautifully wired automobile will nevertheless have problems if everything is not properly grounded. Don't go the effort of installing a quality wire harness only to neglect proper grounding.

Connect a ground strap or cable (minimum of a 4-gauge wire) from the negative battery terminal to the automobile chassis (frame). Connect a ground strap from the engine to the chassis (frame). Do not rely upon the motor mounts to make this connection. Connect a ground strap from the engine to the body.

Rough installation

Caution: Disconnect the power from your vehicle by removing the negative battery cable from the battery.

Note: Make no wire connections or permanent mounting of any kind at this time. Position the computer and sensors in their intended locations.

Drill a 1-5/8" hole for the firewall grommet near the computer for the engine group and tail section to pass through.

With the factory covers and no typical distributor, the LT-1 style injection makes for a neat installation and no worries about distributor to firewall clearance.

Route the engine group and tail section through the hole. Push the grommet (already installed on the harness) into the hole until it is seated.

Route the dash group over to the driver's side of the car.

Route the sensor group to the place where the sensors will be mounted.

HARNESS ATTACHMENT

Note: Harness routing will be a time-consuming task. Taking your time will enhance the beauty of your installation. Please be patient.

Permanently mount computer. You should mount the parts (sensors, relays, etc.) that will be used for your engine at this time. These parts will vary by application.

Mold harness groups to the contour of the dash, engine, frame, etc. Remember to route the harness away from sharp edges, exhaust pipes, hinges, and moving parts.

Attach harness groups to your automobile with clips or ties starting at the computer and working your way outward.

Note: Do not tighten tie wraps or mounting devices at this time. Make all harness attachments LOOSELY.

When used every 1-1/2" or so on the visible areas of the harness, colored plastic wire ties make a very attractive assembly. Otherwise, a tie installed in other areas every 6" or so will hold the wires in place securely. *Remember To Take Your Time.*

WHAT ABOUT MY FORD?

If you're not a Bow Tie Guy and want to run a Ford engine with EFI in your hot rod, then the harness options are more limited. The connectors used on the Ford system are unique and not readily available to aftermarket companies manufacturing wiring harness kits.

If you want to equip your Ford V-8 with factory style fuel injection, there are two options:

With a little polish and chrome plate, either style of TPI can make for a very flashy engine compartment.

either adapt a complete G.M. system and G.M. computer to the Ford engine, or buy a wiring harness kit and any other necessary accessories from Ford Motorsport.

The kits and parts available from Ford Motorsport make it possible to add a fuel injected 302 or 351 cubic inch engine to your street rod or specialty vehicle. Like G.M., Ford has manufactured both mass-air and speed-density fuel injection systems over the years. The "kit" available from Ford Motorsport is designed to aid you in installing a mass-air type system on a small-block 302 or 351 engine. This is essentially the same system used on Mustang GTs from 1989 to 1993, and in California GTs in 1988. The "kit" is actually a series of Ford part numbers, all listed in the Motorsport catalog, starting with a main harness, part number M-12071-C302, which con-

Throttle Body Injection 60101 and 60201

Main Computer	1227747
Brake Switch	25524845
Neutral Safety Switch	1570538
Manifold Absolute Pres.Sensor	16137039
Elec. Spark Control Module	16128261
Fuel Pump Relay (Style 1)	14078915
Fuel Pump Relay (Style 2)	14089936
Coolant Temperature Sensor	25036979
Knock Sensor	10456018
Oxygen Sensor	AFS 21
Oil Pressure Switch	25036553
Vehicle Speed Sensor	PPP 60115
Distributor to Coil Wiring	12039177
Coil Power/Tach Pigtail	12101896
EGR Solenoid	1997111

MAF Tuned Port Injection 60102 and 60202

Main Computer	1227165 or 16198259
Brake Switch	25524845
Neutral Safety Switch	15679680
Elec. Spark Control Module	16128261
Fuel Pump Relay (Style 1)	14078915
Fuel Pump Relay (Style 2)	14089936
Coolant Temperature Sensor	25036979
Knock Sensor	10456018
Oxygen Sensor	AFS 21
Mass Airflow Sensor	14094712
Mass Airflow Power Relay	10067925
Mass Airflow Burn off Relay	10094701
Oil Pressure Switch	25036553
Vehicle Speed Sensor	PPP 60115
Distributor to Coil Wiring	12039177
Coil Power/Tach Pigtail	12101896
EGR Solenoid	1997111

MAP - TUNED PORT INJECTION 60103 AND 60203

Main Computer	1227730 or 16198262
Brake Switch	25524845
Neutral Safety Switch	15679680
Manifold Absolute Pres.Sensor	16137039
Fuel Pump Relay (Style 1)	14078915
Fuel Pump Relay (Style 2)	14089936
Coolant Temperature Sensor	25036979
Knock Sensor	10456126
Oxygen Sensor	AFS 21
Oil Pressure Switch	25036553
Vehicle Speed Sensor	PPP 60116
Distributor to Coil Wiring	12039177
Coil Power/Tach Pigtail	12101896
EGR Solenoid	1997111

MEM-CAL CHIPS

Mild 350 (Street Legal)	64010
Mild 305 (Street Legal)	64020
Hot 350	64030
LT-1	64050

NOTE: These chips will only work with the MAP Tuned Ports (5.0ℓ & 5.7ℓ) All mem-cal chips are street-legal.

Failure to use the right parts (with exactly the right part number) is a common cause of installation problems. Painless provides this list to ensure anyone who buys their kit also uses the right computer, sensors and related parts. Note, the 64020 chip is no longer available.

nects to the computer, sensors and relays.

Find the right donor

Depending on how complete your donor engine is, you may also need the sensor and relay package, number M-12071-D302; and an engine harness and controls package, M-12071-E302.

Finally, Ford sells the correct computer and mass-air-flow sensor with a snorkel and bracket. Before buying a computer for the Ford system you need to know whether you will be running a manual or automatic transmission If the transmission will be an automatic, you need to know exactly which automatic transmission it will be. The kit is intended to have an input from a vehicle speed sensor.

The instructions for the Ford fuel injection kit include warnings similar to those seen in the G.M. kit from Painless. The Ford people insist you not weld on the car without first disconnecting the multi-pin plug to the computer.

They also remind us that leaded fuel will damage the oxygen sensors and that the grounds must be made to paint and rust free surfaces.

Unlike the G.M. system, the Ford computer does not use an easily replaced PROM. Changes to injector pulse width or ignition curves can, however, be made with the Extreme Performance Engine Control system. Essentially this system allows the well-informed user with his or her own laptop computer to change the calibration of the computer, thus allowing more flexibility (and more work) than simply changing a PROM on a G.M. system.

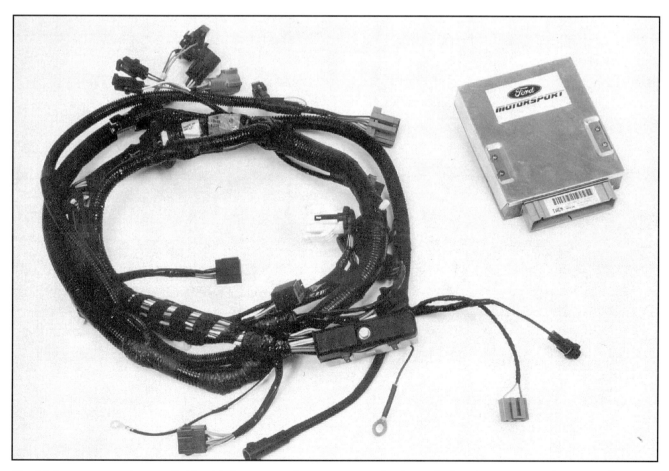

Ford Motorsport makes available this harness and computer, and a host of related parts, to make it easy for nearly anyone to install an EFI small block Ford motor in their car or truck. Unlike G.M. systems, Ford computers can only be altered by someone with access to the Extreme Performance Engine Control System.

Chapter Eight

The Future

Simplex

Considering the increasing complexity of modern automotive electrical systems that require wiring harnesses with hundreds of individual wires, it's not too surprising that an American company would design and produce a complete electrical harness that relies on only two small wires to run the engine and accessories, turn on the headlights, turn signals or any accessory.

The key to the whole system is a new technology known as "multiplexing." Often used

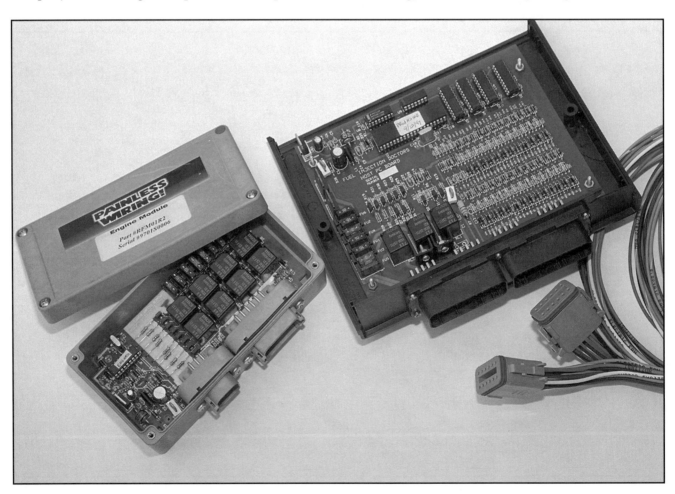

Simplified and computerized, Simplex relies on a host computer like that on the right, to signal three or more "servers" like the one on the left.

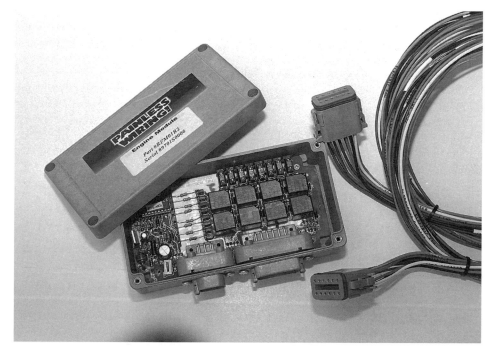

light(s). Only the signal to turn the lights on and off would actually move through a light wire that runs from the main computer to the front or rear server. The dash lights are "served" not by a separate server but by the host computer.

As currently produced, this new system from Painless has enough potential circuits to accommodate nearly any accessory. Because the server boxes are sealed from the ele-

As you can see each server has eight relays, one for each circuit, and the same number of fuses.

in computer and telephone systems, multiplexing allows one wire to carry a number of discrete, pulsed, signals. By using one "host" computer under the dash, connected by one or two small wires to an engine, a front and rear "server," the need for an enormous wiring harness is eliminated.

What it is

Though similar systems have been used in aircraft, Painless Wiring is the first aftermarket company to bring a complete multiplexing wiring harness to market. Known as Simplex, this new system eliminates 75% of the wires in a conventional wiring harness. The new Simplex harness from Painless is both lighter and much less complex than anything seen on automobiles before.

When the driver turns on the headlights, the pulsed signal is sent from the host computer to the front server. The actual current to run the lights goes from the battery to the front server, through a fuse in the server box, to the headlights. Likewise, the power for the taillights or back up lights would move from the battery to the rear server, through a fuse, and on to the

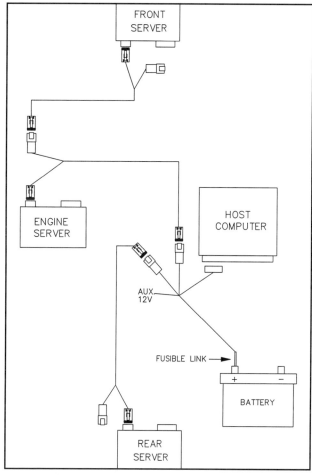

A simplified schematic. In reality there are two signal wires that run between the host and each server, and a power wire for each server.

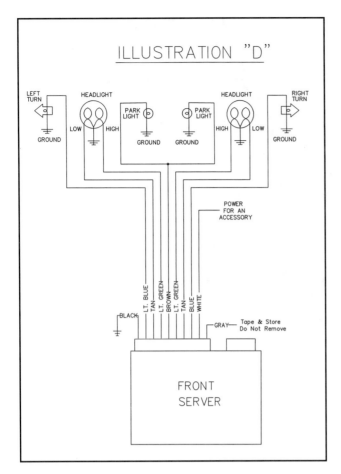

ILLUSTRATION "D"

The front server takes care of the front lights and blinkers. The engine has its own dedicated server.

ments this system can be used for virtually any application, including off-road use.

Plug and play

One of the major advantages of the system is the plug-in design. Each module (hosts and servers) simply plugs into the others. Each server has eight possible functions that are controlled by 10 amp relays for long lasting, dependable service. If the system needs to be expanded, all you have to do is plug in another server and eight more circuits become available.

With minor programming of the main computer up to 240 different functions can be operated at a time.

Trouble-shooting aids are a built-in function of this new system. In case of trouble, each server has a limp home feature that allows necessary functions to operate individually from the rest of the system. By activating the limp home

mode many functions, including the lights, flashers, engine functions and many more, may be operated.

Built in security

The remote control security system is an integral part of the Simplex system. By pressing a button all major engine functions are shut down. If an intruder tries to enter the car while the system is armed, the horn sounds and the lights flash.

Though modern wiring harness kits are as easy to install as possible, the unique design of the Simplex system makes installation simpler still. No longer do you have to run a harness with multiple wires to the front and rear of the car.

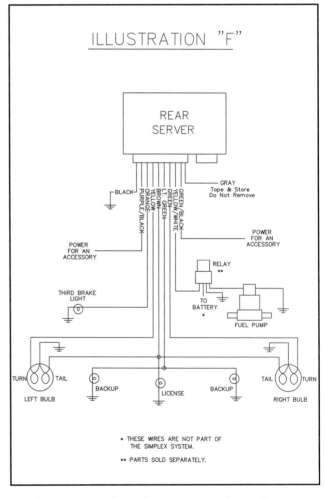

ILLUSTRATION "F"

As the name implies, the rear server "serves" every-thing in the back of the car including the fuel pump.

Installation

All that's required to install the Simplex system is to mount the main host computer under the dash, install the servers, run the signal wires, and wire the servers to the lights, engine and accessories.

One server mounts under the hood to serve the engine, and another server is located on either end of the vehicle. Two 18 gauge wires must be run from the host, mounted under the dash, to each server. Once the servers and host are connected, a battery hot lead must be run to each server, and the individual circuits must be connected to the server.

Connecting the actual circuits is just a matter of attaching the headlight, turn signal or starter wires to the correct wire in the server.

In terms of cost the Simplex system is more expensive than a conventional harness. But when you consider the ease of installation, the simple upgrades and the built in alarm system the expense seems very reasonable. Though Simplex will be offered for sale to individual vehicle owners, it is an ideal system for the manufacturer of an RV or specialty vehicle, where the easy installation and quick upgrades make it a real money saver.

So if you've wondered, "what comes next," in automotive wiring, the answer is here and it's name is Simplex.

The complete system shows the host, servers for engine, headlight and taillight group, and the alarm system with remotes.

Chapter Nine

Install A Harness

Hands-On: The Model A

This is the hands-on chapter that deals specifically with installing a complete wiring harness. The start to finish installation included here is performed on a Model A roadster. We discuss the choice of a harness, changes that must be made to the harness kit, and the installation itself. Though this vehicle is classified as a street rod or hot rod, the lessons learned here apply to the harness installation in your vehicle - whether that vehicle is a new truck or old classic. Because two

Dennis Overholser (on the right) and Greg Ducato size up the job of installing the wiring harness in Greg's Model A. Because the car is very basic with minimalist accessories, Dennis recommended the basic 12 circuit street rod harness.

Dennis determines where the fuse block should mount. He goes so far as to put Greg in the car to ensure that Greg's feet don't run into the fuse block in the proposed location.

This installation illustrates the fact that it's tough to build one harness kit to fit all street rod applications. The specific equipment on the Model A requires a few changes to the kit. As Dennis Overholser from Painless, the man in charge of the installation explains, "We are going to cut off the standard ignition switch plug,

This is the fuse block for the 12 circuit harness, and the mounting bracket that still needs to be located up under the dash.

and sometimes three people worked on the Model A, the ideal installation sequence described below isn't exactly what happened as Dennis and Greg worked on this all-American hot rod.

GETTING STARTED

The vehicle chosen for the hands-on installation is a Model A roadster belonging to Greg Ducato, owner of Phoenix Transmission in Weatherford, Texas. Greg bought the rolling chassis at a swap meet and then added a reproduction Brookville roadster body.

The harness kit being installed is a 12 circuit wiring harness assembly from Painless Wiring, part number 10101. This is a basic street rod wiring kit with 12 circuits, meant for fairly basic cars without accessories like power windows or door locks. This kit comes complete with a pigtail harness designed for a column-mounted G.M. ignition and turn signal switch. (A "pigtail" harness is a sub-harness, like the harness that runs from the turn and ignition switches and then plugs into the main harness.)

Planning plays a big part in any wiring harness installation and before starting the job

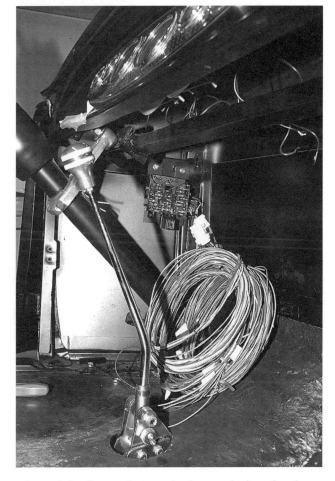

One of the first tasks is to find a good place for the fuse block and permanently mount it up and out of the way.

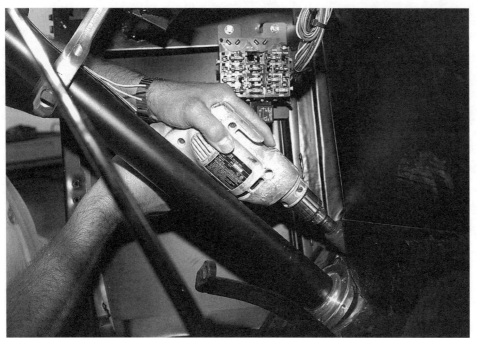

Here you see the drill and 1-1/4 inch hole saw cutting a hole in the firewall for the harness to pass through. The idea is to make the installation neat while leaving the wires accessible.

designed for an ignition switch mounted on the column, and then extend and run the wires over to the universal ignition switch, which will be hidden up under the dash. And we have to make some similar changes for the turn signal wires because this column only has raw wires coming out of the column."

Another example of necessary changes is the electric fuel pump, which will require a modification of the harness because there is no dedicated circuit for the fuel pump.

By planning for modifications like these early in the project there are no surprises and no need to go back after the harness is installed to add a circuit or extend a group of wires.

The actual installation goes like this:

1. Determine where the fuse block should be located and how to mount the fuse block mounting plate. In this case the fuse block will hang off the inner body brace under the dash on the left side.

Note: in general it is easiest to mount the fuse block on the left side of the car though Painless makes harness extension kits that make it easy to mount the fuse block on the passenger side.

2. Mark and drill holes for the sheet metal screws that will mount the fuse block mounting plate.

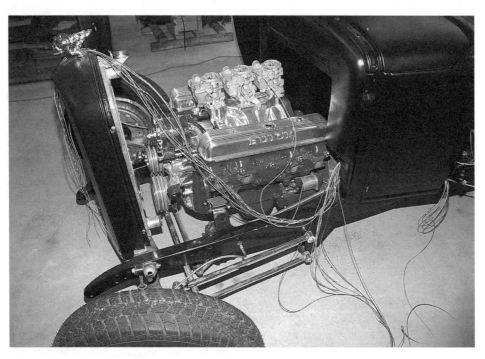

Part of the rough installation includes routing the engine and headlight wires through the firewall and then grouping them into the various sub-groups.

3. Screw the mounting bracket to the body brace and mount the fuse block to the bracket.

4. Decide where to bring the engine wires out of the body and through the firewall. Dennis explains that when trying to decide where the wires should come through the firewall the considerations are, "accessibility and aesthetics. I try to hide the wires as much as possible, but you still need to be able to get at them."

In the case of the Model A, there's a lip on the body just above where the steering column goes through the body. Dennis decides to bring the wires through just below this lip and goes on to explain the decision. "Before you run the harness outside the body through the firewall you must decide where to run the harness for the taillights. In this case, we are going to run them inside the body along the floor pan and into the trunk area. This will make for an easier installation and less chance of damage to the wires. The wires are better protected inside the car and it keeps the frame cleaner in a visual sense.

The other option is to run the taillight wires outside through the firewall and then down along the frame. This decision needs to be made early in the project because it affects which wires go out through the firewall."

5. Drill a 1-1/4 inch hole in the firewall with a hole saw and install the rubber grom-

The kit from Painless provides more than enough wire, so Dennis trims excess wire from the headlight group, out ahead of the front axle.

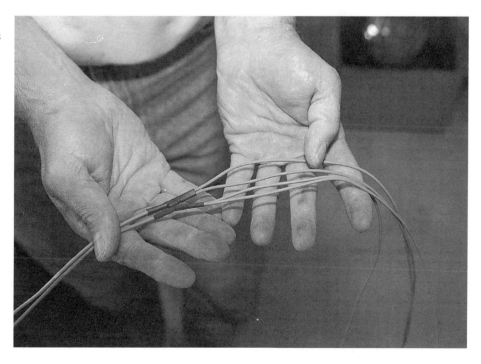

These are the splices in the headlight wires, where a single high or low beam wire splits to power two headlights. Dennis will cut these and move the splices closer to the body.

121

met. The grommet comes with the kit and will prevent chafing of the wires where they pass through the sheet metal firewall.

6. Distribute the wires along the car temporarily. As Dennis explains, "I took the tail section wiring, routed it to the rear and then ran the engine and headlight wiring through the grommet in the firewall. The dash wiring I just left rolled up under the dash for now." All the harnesses in this kit (and all quality kits) are clearly

The wires for the taillight group are "combed" to lie flat and then routed neatly along the floor and held in place with that miracle material - duct tape.

tagged and easy to identify. Dennis cuts some of the excess off the headlight wires and lays them over the radiator.

Note: the headlight wires for this kit are a full 22 feet long. The splices in the headlight and parking light wires, where one wire splits and becomes two, are placed well out into the harness. On a short car like this Model A they end up being out past the end of the frame. So you have to either cut and splice them shorter, or pull some of the wire back up under the dash and neatly tie-wrap it in place.

7. Mount the dimmer switch, which is mounted to the floor in this case. Sometimes it's easier to do this before the fuse box is in place.

8. With the dimmer switch mounted, plug in the small pigtail harness from the switch to the main harness. The plug in at the end of this pigtail fits most dimmer switches, whether they are column-mount or floor-mount style.

Note: color matched duct tape is a good way to hold sub-harnesses in place up against the inner body. The upholstery, once it's installed, will hold the wires there permanently.

9. Make modifications to the harness needed for

Before being grouped into harnesses the wires for the back of the car are simply separated and run past the trunk lid.

122

the alternator. This car uses a one-wire alternator so there is no need for the exciter wire. Instead, this ignition-on wire is run to the back of the car with the taillight group and used to power the fuel tank sender. It's interesting to note that instead of running new wires and circuits to components like the fuel pump Dennis chooses instead to adapt a wire intended for a different circuit that's not in use. You have to be sure that the adapted wire or

Greg will rely on a large diameter electric cooling fan to keep the old Nailhead cool and healthy. The cooling fan is powered by a relay, which in turn is controlled by a sensor in the engine.

this particular hot rod. This Model A differs from the ideal hot rod the wiring harness is designed for. As mentioned, there is no wire for the electric fuel pump. Dennis decides that because the car will have no heater or air conditioning one of these wires should be used to provide power for the electric fuel pump. The 14 gauge wire, black with white stripe, that is part of the engine group normally provides power to the A/C compressor. In this case it will be routed from the fuse block to a toggle switch under the dash, then out the firewall, and finally down along the frame to the fuel pump mounted under the car.

Another adaptation is needed because of the unique fuel "sending unit" used with this car. For safety reasons the Model A body manufactured by Brookville uses a fuel cell rather than a gas tank. The cell is filled with foam so a standard fuel sender won't work. Instead the fuel cell uses a solid state "fuel gauge sender" with three wire connections: an ignition-on power wire, a ground and the sender. In this case the ignition-on power will come from a white 14 gauge wire in the engine group that is normally used as the exciter wire for

The electric cooling fan is mounted on the back side of the radiator (the preferred placement) with special plastic pins. Soft rubber pads are mounted between the fan housing and the radiator.

circuit is heavy enough to handle the load that will be placed on it. Also, as noted earlier, changes like these should be planned out early in the project.

The taillight group now includes six wires: taillights, left blinker/brake, right blinker/brake, fuel gauge sender, fuel gauge power, and the third brake light (which isn't used in this situation).

10. "Comb" the wires for the taillight group. This group of wires should lay

The headlights are mounted in buckets, which are modified to accept the braided stainless hose which will house the wires.

down flat like a ribbon. By combing them you can get them to lay nice and neat and flat. Dennis lays the wires out on the floor, over against the lip of the body, and uses black duct tape to hold the wires in place. When this taillight sub-harness gets past the rear of the seat it is split into two smaller groups; two of the wires (ignition-on power and the wire to the "fuel sender") are run up to the top of the fuel cell and the other four run down through the floor just above the rear axle, through a grommet in the body and then run to the back to feed the brake and taillights. Before finishing with these wires Dennis runs a ground from the seat base bolt to the fuel sending unit.

11. Now it's time to do more sorting of the wires that come out of the firewall. Dennis separates out the wires for the alternator, starter, engine sensors, coil and distributor. It is determined at this time where each sensor will be located and how the wires will be routed.

12. The wires are run to the alternator output terminal (this is a one-wire alternator) and temperature sending unit. After cutting to length, Dennis crimps a terminal on both and hooks them up. For now, he wraps and ties off the distributor

The neutral safety switch is mounted on the shift linkage. The switch is placed in series with the wire for the S terminal on the starter.

wires (incudes the coil and tach wire) because there is no distributor in the car yet.

As Dennis attaches the terminals he describes the right way to do the crimping, "When you're using a terminal with a split at the top of the barrel, and a crimper with a male and female 'die,' always put the male part of the die at the bottom, opposite the split in the connector, otherwise you open up the split when you crimp the wire."

At this time the two wires to the neutral safety switch, part of the engine harness group, are run underneath to the switch mounted on the after-market shift linkage.

13. The oil pressure sender is installed (you have to be sure the sender is matched to the gauge). The wire is run to the sender and a terminal is installed.

14. On the left side of the engine Dennis separates out the two wires for the starter. One of these (the 10 gauge red wire) is hot all the time, it is the main power feed to the fuse box. Dennis puts a fusible link in this circuit, between the big starter terminal and the wire itself. The other wire (12 gauge purple) is the wire that powers the solenoid.

Note: Though "fusible link" wire with a lower melting point is available from a good auto parts store, in a pinch a fusible link can be made up of standard copper wire two sizes

The alternator is a G.M. design modified to function as a one-wire unit. The temperature sender is also mounted for the electronic gauge.

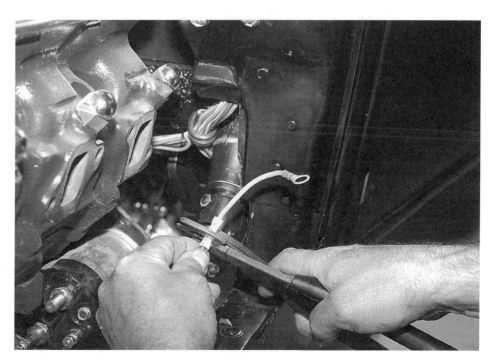

Before attaching the main power lead from the fuse block Dennis puts a fusible link in the wire. Two sizes smaller than the wire it is mounted in, this "fuse" will melt before the larger wire is damaged.

smaller than the circuit it's being installed in.

15. Separate out the wires for the headlight group, run them along the inside of the left frame rail and clamp them into place.

16. Clamp in place the harness containing wires for the fuel pump (mentioned earlier), the brake light switch (two wires), and the starter neutral safety switch (two wires). These wires were separated out from the rest when Dennis sorted the wires that were routed through the firewall.

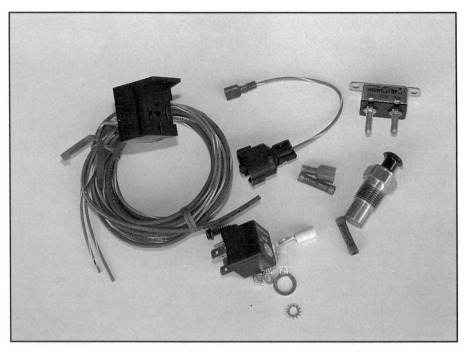

The Painless kit is used to ease installation of the cooling fan. Included are the relay with bracket, temperature sender (available in 2 temperatures) and the circuit breaker.

Note: with the brake master cylinder mounted under the floor the only brake light switch you can use is the hydraulic style. Painless and some others make these with a lower pressure threshold (about 25% less pressure than an OEM switch) so you're sure to get brake lights even with a light pedal application.

17. Next comes the installation of the electric cooling fan. First, the grille shell is removed so Dennis can find the best location for the fan. It is mounted with the small tie-lock type of plastic pins that came with the fan kit, with a small rubber cushion block placed between the actual fan housing and the surface of the radiator.

Note: as a general rule the fan should be located 2/3 of the way to the top of the radiator, because that's where the majority of the heat is. If possible use a puller fan, not a pusher, that way the fan doesn't get in the way of the air moving over the radiator.

Dennis likes to see the electric sensor mounted in the intake manifold near the thermostat, to sense the temperature of the water as it leaves the engine headed for the radiator. You need

Here you can see the installed headlight bucket, the stud for the stainless "hose" and the wires for the headlight and parking lights.

to have a good match between the engine thermo-stat and the sensor rating. Note: the kit used to power the fan is kit #30102 which includes a relay, the sensor (available in two temperatures) and a circuit breaker.

18. Install the relay kit. Normally the relay itself is mounted on the core support next to the radiator, but for this car we will mount it under the car, with the attached bracket screwed to the frame. The two heavy wires are for the load side, the two light wires for the control side. The heaviest of the heavy wires, the 12 gauge from the #30 terminal, goes to battery power, right to the top starter stud if possible. The idea is to be sure it doesn't draw its power through the fuse block. Number 87, the other heavy wire, goes to the fan itself. Numbers 85 and 86 are the trigger or control wires. One is run to a power source at the fuse block and the other is the ground wire, which runs directly to the sensor. It doesn't matter in this situation which of the two wires run to power and which to ground.

19. Dennis runs the headlight harness along the frame to just behind the front cross member, where it is clamped to the frame. Just past this clamp the harness is split to the left and right side wires.

The headlight wires run through braided stainless housings from the frame to the headlight bucket. To attach the flexible stainless tubes to the headlights the original buckets had to be drilled out to accept the threaded connectors. Two small fabricated brackets mount the lower end of the braided cable to the frame.

20. Next, the headlight buckets are installed and the wires are routed into the buckets. Once the buckets are in place Dennis runs four wires into each bucket: high and low beam, and park and turn signal wires (park and turn signal lights may be added to this car at a later date). The headlight buckets will ground through the swivel and mounting bolt.

21. The wiring for the gauges is done on the bench. On some cars gauges can be pulled out as an assembly. With the Model A the gauges had to be removed as individual components, then loose-

Looking down onto the left frame rail you can see how the harness is run and clamped onto the rail itself.

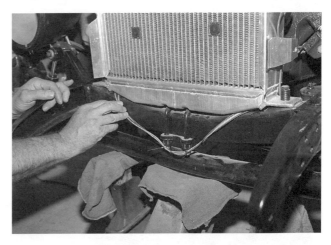

In front the wires run under the edge of the radiator, down to the spring clamp and then over to the other side.

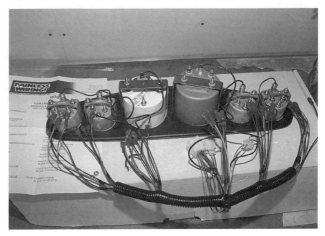

On the Model A we had to pull the gauges from the dash and assemble them temporarily on the bench, then install the Painless gauge harness.

Before plugging the gauge harness into the main harness, the correct plug - and all the necessary pins - must be installed on the main harness.

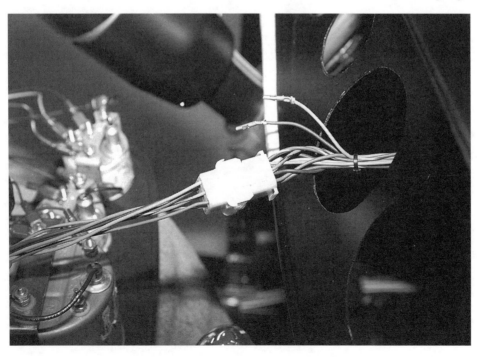

This close up shows the two plugs, one attached to the gauge harness and the other to the main harness, and a few of the individual pins from the main harness that have not been installed in the plastic plug-in yet.

ly reassembled on the bench in the correct order, determined by the location of the connectors in the Painless wiring harness. With the gauges mounted loosely in the grille and flipped over (check the photos to relieve confusion) slip-fit adapters are screwed on the studs at the back of the gauges. Then all the wires in the dash harness are plugged in to the gauges so Dennis is sure all the wires fit correctly. Wiring the tachometer is a pretty straightforward situation, but before deciding which wires go where on the back of the electric VDO speedometer it's necessary to check the instructions that came with the speedometer.

The dash harness used on this car, which runs from the gauges to the main harness, is an option. You can simply connect the individual wires from the main harness to the gauges. Using a dash harness makes the whole installation easier because now you can wire the gauges on the bench, (instead of doing it up under the dash) unplug the harness, install the gauges, and then pretty much just plug in the harness.

There are some extra wires in the dash harness, for indicator, which might be added later, so we tie-wrap the extra wires out of the way before disassembling the harness from the gauges prior to installation in the car.

22. Once we know the gauge harness matches up correctly to the gauges, the gauges can be reinstalled in the dash. Connecting the pigtail harness for the gauges to the main harness is a little extra work, because the main harness does not have a plug-in installed to match the plug-in on the gauge harness. The answer is to cut off the excess wire on the main harness and install the small round female terminals on the end of each wire. Once the female connectors are installed on the wire ends each one is installed into the plastic housing that matches

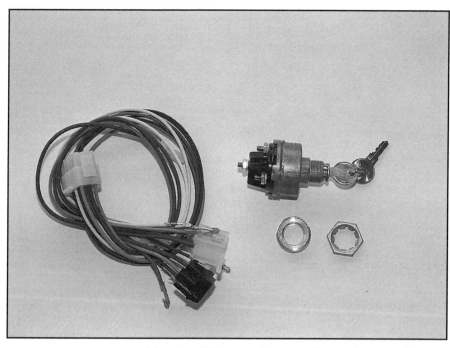

The pigtail harness shown is designed to interface with the stock ignition switch and turn signal switch on a G.M. column. Instead Greg is going to use the universal type switch shown on the right.

up to the one used on the gauge harness. The wires are installed so the color codes on the main harness match the codes on the gauge harness.

Dennis also adds a ground wire from the body to the gauge harness to ensure proper gauge operation.

23. The next step is to install the pigtail harness that plugs into the main harness and runs to the ignition switch and turn signal switch. The 10101 kit comes with a pigtail harness designed to plug into the stock ignition and turn signal switches mounted on a late model G.M. column.

The column in the Model A is a G.M. column but there is no ignition switch. So Dennis snips off the plug for the G.M. ignition switch and installs ring terminals on each wire. Next, the wires are attached to the threaded terminals on the back of the universal style ignition switch before the switch is mounted up under the dash.

24. The turn signal switch presents another challenge. Not

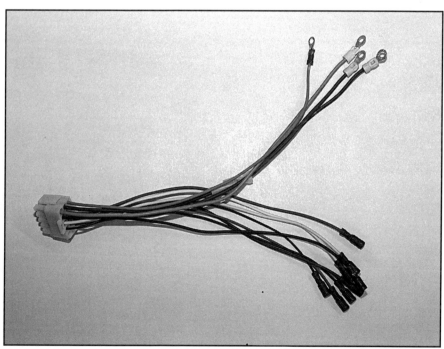

This is the pigtail used for ignition and turn signal switches after its been modified. ring terminals are for the ignition switch while the bullet connectors are for the turn signal switch.

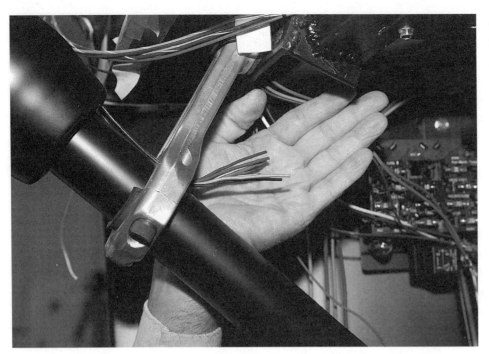

This shot shows how short the wires were cut off coming out of the turn signal switch.

only is there no plug-in on the column, the wires coming out of the turn signal switch have been cut quite short. Dennis solves the problem by first installing male bullet connectors (because they are smaller and less bulky than some other designs) on the wires coming out of the column. Then the plug-in for the G.M. turn signal switch is snipped off the pigtail harness and female bullet connectors are crimped onto the individual wires. Now it's just a matter of connecting the right pigtail wire to the correct wire coming out of the turn signal switch - all made easier by the wiring diagram provided in the Painless instructions.

25. The wires for the headlight switch are already attached to the main harness. Because we are again using a universal style switch, Dennis cuts off the excess wire, installs four connectors and then screws them to the correct terminals.

26. The Painless Wiring main harness provides two purple wires that normally connect to the neutral safety switch on the steering column. In this case the neutral safety switch is located on the shift linkage. Instead of running the two purple wires to the column-mounted neutral safety switch, Dennis put the new neutral safety switch in series, with the purple wire that runs from the ignition switch to the S terminal on the sole-

Dennis crimps a bullet connector on the end of each short wire, the wires will be mated up to the wires in the pigtail harness according to the wiring schematic in the instruction manual. These connectors work well in this situation because they don't take up much room.

noid to energize the solenoid. But there must still be a circuit through the two purple wires meant for the factory neutral safety switch so Dennis simply put a female connector on one and a male on the other and plugged them together.

27. At this point it's important to understand the design of this harness: the circuits for the compressor (black with white stripe) and for the cooling fan, (grey with white stripe) are part of the accessory section, each one has two ends that are part of the harness in the car. They have two ends so that the customer can install a switch in the circuit to control the A/C compressor or cooling fan. Dennis explains that, "people get confused because sometimes after installing the harness the cooling fan won't work, the reason is the two grey wires with white stripe must either run through a switch or be connected together, otherwise there is an open circuit."

One of the last jobs is to install the sender for the cooling fan at the front of the cylinder head, which leaves Greg with just a few more jobs to do. Like hooking up the distributor and fabricating a battery box to fit just behind the gas tank.

Surveying the nearly-finished harness installation, Dennis repeats the advice offered earlier, "This job turned out nice and neat with no big headaches because we followed the directions and we took our time from start to finish."

The sensor for the cooling fan is mounted in the right cylinder head, the other smaller sensor is for the temperature gauge.

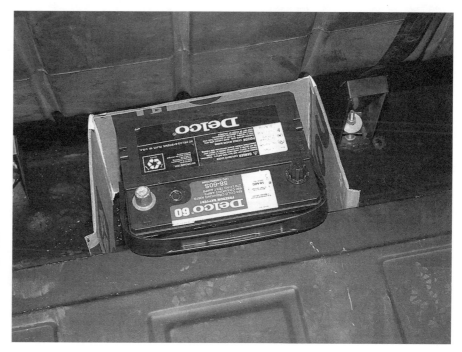

The cardboard represents the battery box Greg will fashion to mount the battery just behind the gas tank.

Chapter Ten

Tips & Trouble Shooting

They're all the same, only different

The idea of this chapter is to provide guidelines for buying a complete harness, along with some simple tips for anyone installing a wiring kit or doing a re-wiring job. The installation tips are broken down by category: trucks and

4X4s, late model cars, American classic cars and competition vehicles. Comments regarding the wiring of a hot rod are included in Chapter Nine, where we wire a Model A from start to finish.

Direct current electricity works the same

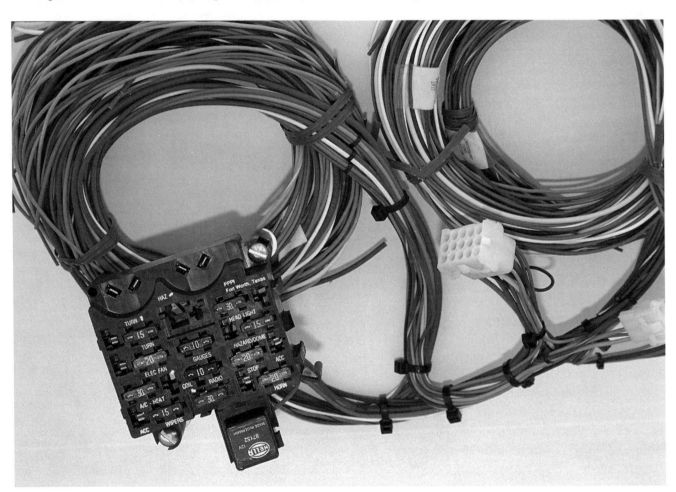

The harness you choose should reflect the vehicle's end use: competition, classic, off road or street rod. Be

sure the harness has enough circuits and features to match the intended use.

in a 4X4 as it does in a hot rod Camaro. Nearly any vehicle will be equipped with the same basic ignition, horn and lighting circuits. This is not to say, however, that the harness kit you buy for a truck should be the same one you buy for a Firebird, especially if the Firebird in question is a competition vehicle that only gets driven one quarter mile at a time.

The idea is to help you buy the best product, be it a complete harness or a auxiliary fuse block, and then provide guidance as to the best way to install that product.

This 18-circuit harness assembly meant for Chevy and GMC trucks comes in two versions ('73 to '87 and '67 to '72) and features a factory-style bulkhead connector. Painless Wiring

WHICH HARNESS TO BUY

Before buying a harness you need to determine how the vehicle will be used and how many circuits you need. A competition car needs a different harness than a street car. A fancy sedan with power windows, air conditioning and the monster stereo will need a more complex harness than a stripped down Model A like that seen in Chapter Nine.

If you're buying a harness for a true street rod, consider the ignition switch location before buying the harness. If your ignition switch is on the G.M. column, does the harness include the correct plug-in for that switch location?

A number of companies make harness kits designed for specific applications, from full race to OEM duplicates. The best one for your car or truck depends on what you intend to do with the vehicle.

When you buy a wiring harness look for a company that's been in business for a long time. One with a proven record for quality and a tech line to help with answers to your questions. A good harness comes with different color codes on

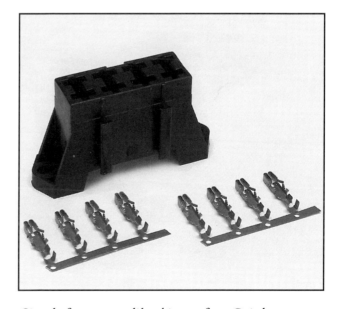

Simple fuse centers like this one from Painless are good for adding extra circuits in situations that don't require relays.

This 8-circuit universal harness assembly is meant for competition use. Each circuit is protected by a fuse and a 30-amp relay. Painless Wiring

This charging circuit shutdown relay is a good way to isolate the ignition circuit from the alternator when the key is shut off - thus preventing any run-on. Painless Wiring

all the different circuits, and durable labels on the wires and groups of wires to make installation as easy as possible. The wires themselves should be high quality multi-strand copper with the best grade of insulation (for more on wire quality see Chapter One).

Should you buy a fuse block or a complete harness kit?

Painless Wiring (and other companies as well) manufactures a fuse box without any wires attached. Each circuit is labeled. The idea is that you can run the wires from the fuse box to the headlight switch, fuel sender or whatever. The cost is considerably less than a full harness kit made up of a fuse box with all the wires already attached. Dave McNurlen, the man who generally answers the Tech Line at Painless, often has people calling about this. "They want to know if they should buy just the fuse box and run their own wires, or if they should buy a complete harness kit with the wires already attached."

"I tell them, 'don't buy just the fuse block and run your own wires, unless you are a pretty good mechanic.' And even if they are a good mechanic, the time they spend running the wires, labeling them and all the rest is not time well spent. You won't have the various sized wires, and your crimps and connections won't be as good as our machine crimps. If you buy a bare fuse block and connect all the wires yourself there will be at least twice as many crimps and many more connections overall. This means more room for corrosion, bad connections and failure in the future.

There's also the question of simply buying enough wire with enough different color codes so you don't duplicate colors as you run the wires in the various circuits. In nearly every case, you will spend an awful lot of time to save only a pretty modest amount of money."

The Roy Hill series of drag race switch panels are designed to mount to the roll bar. Each switch meets military-specifications. Plug-in design allows for quick removal. Painless Wiring

INSTALLATION TIPS

Trucks and 4X4s

Trucks and four wheel drive vehicles are similar both in their overall construction and in the way they are used. These are heavy duty vehicles that see considerable use and abuse, often in dusty, wet conditions.

When buying a harness or wiring kit, some basic guidelines apply. Know ahead of time the kind of accessories the vehicle will have and be sure to buy a harness that will meet your electrical needs. As always, if you intend to run power windows, locks or a similar accessory, be sure the fuse block and harness have enough capacity and specific circuits to handle that load. In the G.M. line, some late model trucks put the ignition switch on the column while others do not. Be sure the harness assembly you buy will interface with your ignition switch type and location.

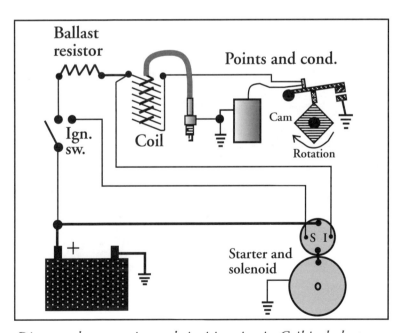

Diagram shows a points-style ignition circuit. Coil includes two windings, primary and secondary. When points open magnetic field created by primary winding collapses on secondary winding, generating a spark. Note the resistor by-pass circuit from starter.

135

Trucks come in various lengths, new and old, full size and mini, with short and long beds. If your truck is a long bed be sure the taillight part of the harness is physically long enough to reach all the way to the license plate light.

Factory four wheel drive trucks often have a light to remind the driver that the transfer case is indeed in the 4X4 mode. The truck harness from Painless does have a provision to operate this light.

Trucks are not only subject to dirt and water, they are often equipped with additional electrical accessories. When installing fog lights, roll bar lights and electric cooling fans, keep in mind the fact that trucks often live in a harsh environment that puts extra demands on the electrical components.

When installing accessories on trucks it might be good idea to use water resistant connec-tors to plug in the lights themselves. And if you decide to use relays to carry the load - always a good idea - consider mounting the relay itself either inside the cab, or at least as high as possible under the hood.

Extra circuits can be added to your truck with an auxiliary fuse block. Like the switches, some of these fuse blocks are available in water resistant models.

Late model cars
If the car you're building or re-wiring is a late model Camaro or a Dodge Dart, the wiring con-siderations are different from a truck or a true hot rod.

First, remember that because these vehicles are relatively new, you have more options when it comes to buying a complete harness. OEM style

Painless Wiring offers this bare fuse block with 12 circuits - each one clearly labeled.

harnesses are available from a variety of sources, including aftermarket companies specializing in particular makes and models. Sometimes you can find an original factory harness for an older vehicle, still in the original box, from one of the specialty shops listed in *Hemmings Motor News*.

An OEM style harness with bulkhead connections at the firewall makes for a much neater wiring installation. Not all OEM style harnesses are the same, however. Some are close to the original harness, some are exact duplicates, and still others might be called "improved."

If you are restoring a car and intend to take it to the show when you're finished, you want a harness that's an exact duplicate of the original. That way you won't loose any points because the wire to the alternator is the wrong color.

The problem with the original harness for older cars is the fact that they probably don't have

enough circuits to handle modern conveniences we all take for granted. Painless Wiring makes a G.M. "muscle car" harness in an OEM style with a bulkhead connection. This improved harness is designed to plug into the factory heater controls, headlight and ignition switches and even the wiper control. In addition this harness offers circuits for air conditioning, power door locks and windows, an electric fuel pump and an electric fan.

If you're building a pro street car, one that's fast but also fully street legal, Painless makes a harness that provides for competition features like electric fuel and water pumps combined with features you need on the street like headlights, turn signals and all the rest.

If you're wiring a late model car it's a good idea to have the factory wiring diagram. No matter how complete the wiring harness you buy is, you will probably end up using parts of the origi-

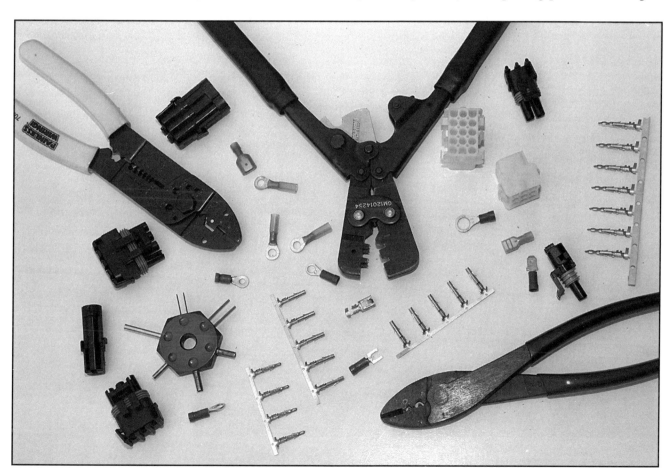

For wiring a car or truck you need a variety of connectors and crimping tools to do a neat, safe wiring job. Plastic plug-in housings require the right connectors which in turn require the correct crimping tool.

Watches and rings belong on the bench, not on your hands as you work.

nal harness. In these situations it's doubly important to know what the original harness did, what all the wire color codes are and exactly which wire went where.

Classic American cars

If you're building or restoring a classic American car, like a '55 Chevy or a '52 Packard, consider again whether or not you need an OEM Style harness to please the judges. Consider too that the original wiring harness on a car from the 1950s doesn't have very many circuits. If you intend to add air conditioning or power windows you need either a newer harness assembly with more circuits or an add-on auxiliary fuse block of some kind, preferably one with relays to handle the heavy loads.

Though strict OEM style harnesses are available, so are more modern harnesses designed specifically for the more popular cars. Painless Wiring and others make a variety of modern harness assemblies for cars like the '55 through '57 Chevrolet. These give you an easy way to provide enough circuits for modern conveniences like air conditioning and power windows.

Not only do modern aftermarket harnesses provide more circuits, they use better insulation and easier to follow color codes in most cases. If the car in question is an old Cadillac, be sure the aftermarket har-

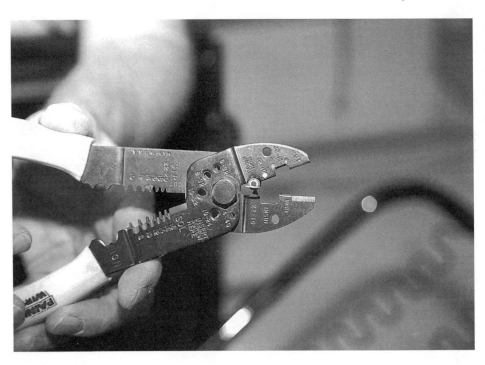

Here you can see how the most common type of crimping tool is used to correctly squeeze a connector, note the male part of the tool is at the bottom while the split in the connector is at the top.

ness you intend to buy is long enough.

The question that often comes up when discussing wiring cars of this vintage is: what to do with the original six volt gauges and accessories. As Dennis Overholser points out in his interview in Chapter One, you need a different solution for the gauges than for the heater motor. An aftermarket voltage converter, to convert from 12 to 6 volts, works fine for the gauges. Things like heater fans, however, that have a heavier amperage draw will have to be converted to 6 volts with a ceramic type of resistor.

Competition vehicles

Competition vehicles have unique electrical needs. Instead of having enough circuits for air conditioning and power door locks, you need enough circuits to handle multiple fuel pumps and an electric water pump. Most of these components draw enough current that you also need to be sure the circuits are designed to handle the load, and that relays are part of the harness design.

Most of the competition kits come with on-off switch panels to control the various circuits. Before buying the kit and panel, figure out where the panel will mount and then find a kit that mounts easily in that location. Some switch panels can be mounted in

more than one way and a few can simply be mounted to the roll bar with two hose clamps. If the driver will be wearing a full fire suit and gloves, be sure the style of switch, rocker or toggle, can be easily operated with gloves on. Be sure the switches you use are all heavy-duty designs with

Dave McNurlen, an ASE certified technician, is the man in charge of the tech line at Painless Wiring.

Heat-shrink tubing comes in various sizes, including these which are large enough for battery cables. Painless Wiring

Weatherpack connectors are a good idea for lights and accessories mounted outside the vehicle. Painless Wiring

tight fitting terminals that won't shake loose in the middle of a race.

As mentioned earlier, if your race car is street legal, then a Street Machine harness from Painless Wiring, or a similar product, might give you the perfect blend of features for the street and strip.

With competition cars that use very simple wiring harnesses there sometimes arises the problem where the car keeps running even though all the switches are turned off. Usually the problem is caused by an electric cooling fan motor that acts as a generator when the engine is shut off, thus providing voltage to the ignition circuit. You can solve a problem like this by running the fan off a relay (which will isolate the circuit) or you can add a diode, which acts as a one-way switch, in the power wire of the offending electric motor. Radio Shack offers a single 6 amp 50 PIV diode #276-1661 that works well in these situations.

Run-on can also be caused by feedback from the alternator's exciter circuit, again in cars with simple ignition switches and wiring schemes. Painless makes a charging system shutdown relay that isolates the alternator when the key is turned off.

TROUBLE SHOOTING

The following is a question and answer session with Dave McNurlen, the man who answers the tech line at Painless Wiring. Before coming to work at Painless Dave spent 20 years as a G.M. technician and is rated as an ASE certified Master Technician.

Before we could get to the most popular questions, and their answers, Dave offered the following two tips for anyone who is installing a harness kit in any type of vehicle.

First, Dave explains that many of the calls to the tech line could be eliminated if people would just read and follow the instructions. "They should take the instructions into the house and read them from cover to cover, before they start to do the wiring job. It will make the job easier and save time in the long run.

The other good idea is to buy or borrow a factory wiring diagram. This doesn't apply to street rods or race cars, but for most of the others it's very helpful if you have some idea what the original harness did. You will probably end up using parts of the original harness in conjunction with the new harness kit so you need to be able to correctly identify the wires and components."

COMMONLY ASKED QUESTIONS

Q: Should I hook up an amp meter or a voltmeter?
A: You should hook up a voltmeter (this subject is also covered in Chapter Four). It's safer, you don't have those big wires running through the dash. Voltmeters are more modern, still have good indication of whether or not the charging circuit is working.
Q : When do I need a ballast resistor?

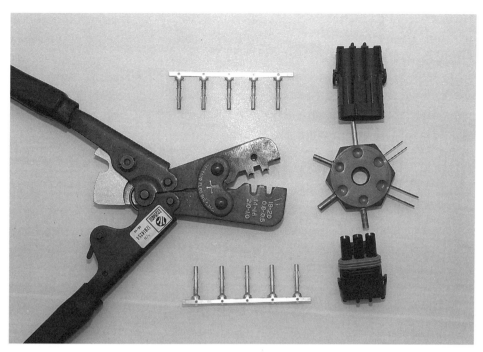

Big crimping tools like this might seem expensive, but they're the best way to neatly crimp the factory-style connectors that crimp onto both the wire and the insulation. You will need the other tool shown to remove the connectors from the plug-in body without damaging the connector itself.

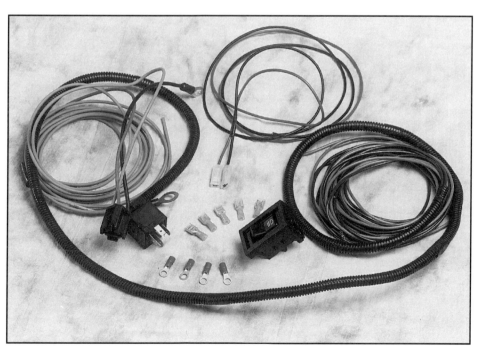

Do a neat, safe job of wiring those auxiliary fog or driving lights with this relay kit. Painless Wiring

A: You need a ballast resistor with a points-type ignition. With electronic ignition you don't need a ballast resistor (with the exception of some Chrysler ignition circuits). Some younger people don't understand the old points type system and why it needs a ballast resistor. They don't understand the bypass circuit either (see the diagram on page 135).

Q: When do I use a relay, what does it do and why can't I just use a switch?

A: Things like cooling fans that draw a lot of amps are hard on switches. Most switches won't handle that much amperage without premature failure. I explain it this way: The relay is the switch for the load, and the switch itself just activates the relay.

Q: Which alternator should I buy and how do I hook it up?

A: You should figure out what the power demands are that you will place on the alternator. There are a lot of options here. Match the alternator to the loads you're going to put on it. There are a number of different circuits, it's confusing and you need to know which alternator you've got and then follow the wiring diagram for that particular alternator (Chapter Two presents a variety of alternator circuits).

Q: Should I buy a one-wire alternator?

A: They seem to need more rpm to energize, to start charging, but you don't know that unless you're watching your voltmeter all the time. The newer CS series alternators from G.M. work well and make good power at very low rpm. The one-wire alternators look pretty, but they're based on the old G.M. alternator so the output is limited

This heavy duty switch panel comes with waterproof push button and two toggle switches, and a harness with weatherpack connectors. Painless Wiring.

compared to the newer designs.

Q: Where's the wire for the brake lights?

A: For many American cars the brake light switch feeds power to the turn signal switch. The brake lights are actually fed through the turn signal switch - the brake and turn signal light or filament are the same thing. (Note, some later cars with separate red and amber brake and turn signal lenses actually run the brake light wire back to the brake light bulbs on either side.)

Q. I've got two cooling fans and the AC compressor on one circuit and I keep blowing fuses. Why can't I just put in a bigger fuse?

A. the circuit will only handle so much current. If you put in a bigger fuse than the circuit is designed for you risk melting the wires in that circuit.

The electric cooling fans should be run off a relay. Mount the relay under the hood, take the power off the starter for example, fuse it with a fusible link, and then run the power to the load side of the relay, through the relay to the fan and ground the other side of the fan.

I tell people to keep all the heavy circuits under the hood so they have shorter load wires, less voltage drop, less chance for wires to get chaffed or cut.

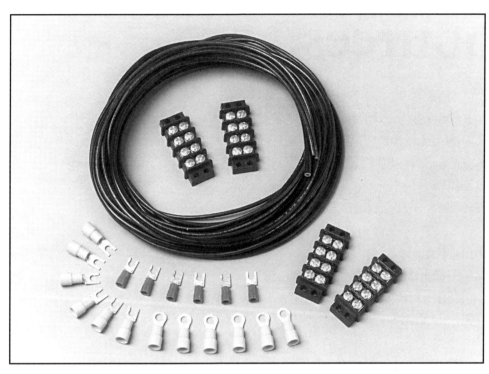

A common problem with fiberglass bodies is establishing enough good grounds. This kit is designed to eliminate that problem. Painless Wiring

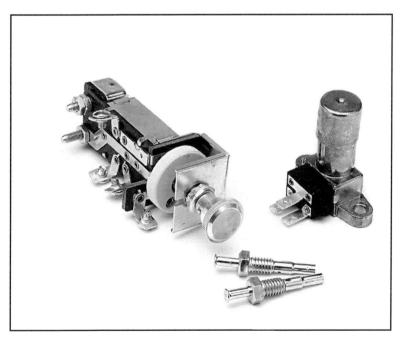

This kit from Painless includes a universal-style headlight switch, one floor-mount dimmer switch and two dome-light switches. Painless Wiring

Sources

Auto Meter Products, Inc.
413 W. Elm St.
Sycamore, IL 60178
815 895 8141
www.autometer.com

Doug Rippie Motorsports
14070 23rd Ave. N.
Plymouth, MN 55447
612 559 7605

Ford Motorsport Performance Equipment
44050 N. Groesbeck Highway
Clinton Township, MI 48036
Tech Line: 810 468 1356

Painless Wiring
9505 Santa Paula
Fort Worth, TX 76116
817 244 6898
Painless Tech Line
 817 560 TECH

Sound Waves
7233 University Ave.
Fridley, MN 55432
612 572 2636
FAX: 612 572 3945

Vintage Air
10305 I.H. 35 N.
San Antonio, TX 78233
800 862 6658